PHOTOGRAPHY JUDGING

FOR **PHOTOGRAPHERS** PHOTOJUDGES **PICTURE EDITORS**

Other books

Photography: History, Art, Technique
Photography - the Definitive Visual History
Photography Judging 1st ed
Photo Insights
Picture Editing
Ang's World
Photo Field Guide
Creativity for Everyone
Digital Photography Step by Step
Digital Photography Essentials
Digital Photographer's Handbook
Complete Digital Photography
Questions & Angswers
Digital Photography: an Introduction
The Complete Photographer
Digital Photography Masterclass
Fundamentals of Photography
Digital Photography Through The Year
How To Photograph Absolutely Everything
Digital Photography
Tao of Photography
Eyewitness Companion: Photography
Picture Editing
Photoshop CS For Photography
Dictionary of Photography & Digital Imaging
Digital Photography
Silver Pixels
KISS Digital Photography
Advanced Digital Photography
Complete Digital Photography
Private Album
Digital Video Handbook
Digital Video: An Introduction

As photographer

The Marco Polo Expedition
Joy of Sex
Walking the Scottish Highlands
Dorset

Contents

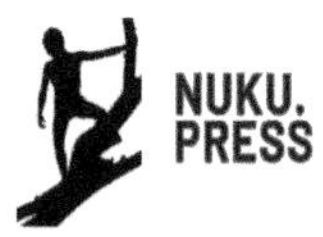

ISBN 978-0-473-55920-5
Fonts used: Barlow, Trirong, Taviraj
Published in New Zealand by AngBookCo an
imprint of Nuku.Press

Introduction

THIS IS A PRACTICAL MANUAL for judging photography in any context. From international competitions, awards and concours to personal projects and educational institutions, it is a unique source. This book can inform and help anyone who judges, evaluates, selects or uses photographs in any capacity.

This book is designed to be an essential guide for photographers of all grades ... and even if they need only to judge their own work.

It also offers essential reading and reference material for those who wish to enter their images to photography competitions, concours, or salons.

Above all, it is designed to be a comprehensive handbook for those who carry any responsibility for judging photographic entries for awards or prizes at any level.

If you are, or have been invited to be, a photography judge this book aims to give you all the information you need to perform your duties with skill, flair, and fairness. With the thousands of competitions, awards, salons, and photo concours that take place around the world, there is a pressing need for a clear, authoritative manual to guide photojudges.

This book aims to be that manual.

Visual references

This book is not full of visual references. The reason is that it's not my purpose to influence - let alone dictate or determine - what works or doesn't work visually or photographically. However, I have included some visual exercises to help the less experienced work on how to analyse, then articulate in words, their visual and visceral responses.

I have worked for 40 years in photography in many capacities: from leading Masters courses at university to beginner workshops, from editing photography magazines to running a picture desk for a national newspaper to consulting for the photo industry. I've also judged extensively. From club competitions to sitting on juries of some of the most important photography awards in the world I've had the pleasure and honour to breathe and talk photography with some of the finest photographers, picture editors and photography judges on the planet.

Certain questions recur; every photography judge on every continent, in every country will be asked a variant of them. It reflects what appears to be a mysterious, unpredictable process and takes many forms:

- 'How do you judge a photograph?'

- 'What makes a photograph good or bad?'

- 'How can you spot the one great photograph from among thousands of others?'

- 'Surely judging photography is totally subjective?'

- 'What's the difference between a good photograph and a bad one?'

- 'How do you know what is a good photo?'

This book is essentially a long answer to those questions. In doing so, I hope to help you become a skilful, subtle, prudent judge of photographs. And that you'll appreciate there's much less subjectivity and more objectivity than you might think.

While being a great picture editor offers no guarantee that you can make great photographs, you can be sure the reverse is true: gaining good picture judging skills confers enormous benefit to any photographer.

May this book improve your photography, and picture judging!

Auckland 2021

NOTE

In this book the term 'picture editing' means "the process of selecting an image best suited to a specific use or purpose", and a picture editor or photojudge is someone engaged in that process. Picture editing is not the same as image editing which is the process of using image manipulation software to alter or process images. Therefore, in this book, 'picture editing' does not mean 'image manipulation'.

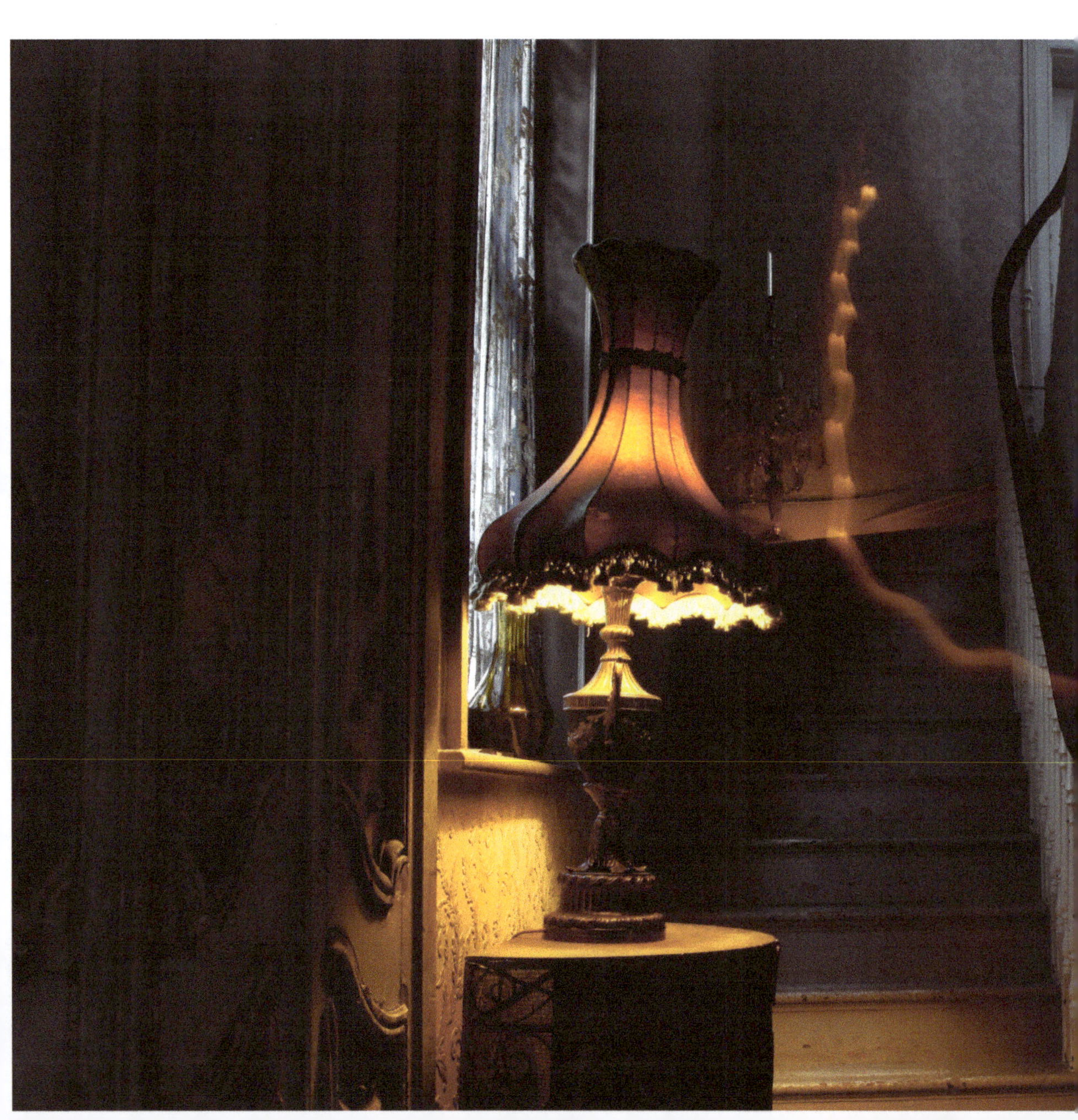

Essentials

Chapter One

Responsibilities

Basic selection strategies

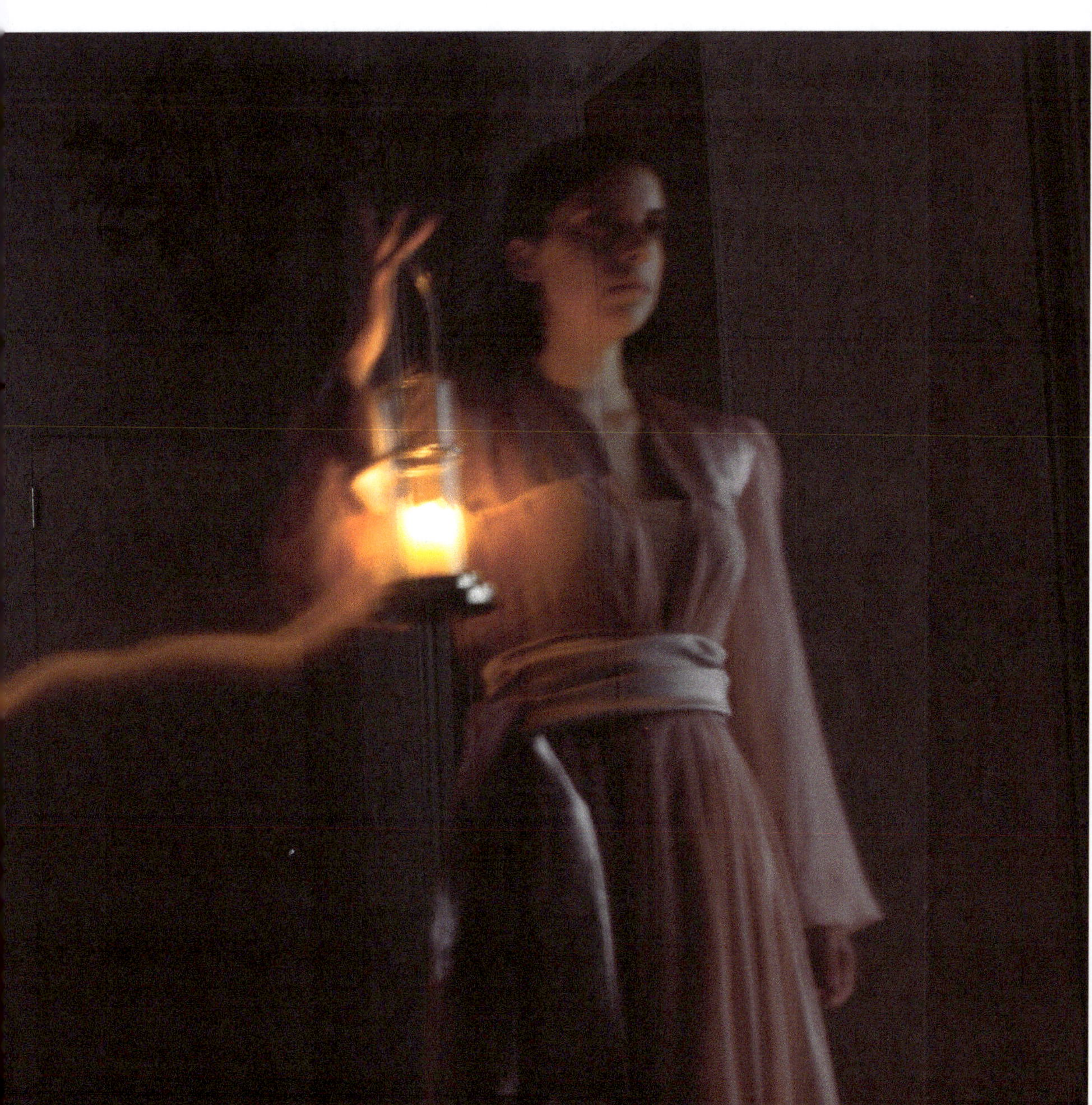

Responsibilities

YOU COULD SAY that anyone who can capture an image has what is needed to judge a photograph. They can see, they have their own tastes, they can express their preferences between what they like or don't like. In short, they can form their own opinion about a photograph. And just about everyone is very willing to express their opinions. However, there is more to judging photography than personal opinion.

Responsibilities

At the very least, everyone can judge their own photographic efforts, if even they never look at anyone else's. Nonetheless, there is a small - but rapidly-growing - number of photographers who take on responsibilities for judging that go beyond their own photographs. A lot further: their judgements may themselves be judged by others, sometimes debated all round the world.

If you are one of these, if you have been asked to judge a photographic award, salon or prize - whether at the local club, regional or even at international level - you take on a big responsibility.

It's a responsibility both to the photographers taking part, and to the competition organisers. It's a responsibility to know what you're doing. Knowing your photography does not automatically make you a photography judge. You have a responsibility to understand the framework of rules, to appreciate the process of judging photographic work; and you take on a wider duty of being an opinion leader in photography.

With the great increase in numbers of awards and prizes for photography, a proportionally big increase in the numbers of judges is needed. Many judges are appointed from the ranks of past winners. Although being a fine photographer does not guarantee the person is a skilled judge of photography, one can learn on the job. Many of the finest picture editors and photojudges have risen from the ranks of photography, gaining experience from looking at, assessing and using images for years until they become expert at assessing images in dynamic, sophisticated and educated ways.

This book won't try to substitute for the experience and knowledge gained from the critical assessment of thousands of all kinds of images and accumulated over many years of working at high levels in book publishing, magazine editing or curating exhibitions.

This book does, however, provide a framework for those who need to acquire the essential skills and understanding to be able to function as a responsible and skilled photojudge.

In addition, there is a great deal of material in this book that will benefit any photographer keen to hone their picture-editing skills. Improving your pictureediting can be the most effective, and cost-efficient way to improve your photography. This extends to improving your chances of winning photographic awards, and getting exhibitions or being published.

How to use this book

This book is split broadly into two parts. The first deals with the fundamentals of judging and understanding how we respond to the image. For example, our assessment of an image may change according to the context of its use or the photographic genre. We will also look at technical issues, discuss images and their uses in different contexts. And we look briefly at the art of sequencing or creating panels of images.

Central to the whole processing of judging and editing is how to select the single winning image out of hundreds or thousands. By 'winning' we mean not only the photograph selected as a prize- or award-winner, but also pictures that will 'win' an honoured position in a photographer's portfolio or web-site.

This first part will be useful to photographers who are working only with their own images as well as helpful to judges and picture editors. However, it is worth saying now that this book is not a guide to image or digital asset management and image workflows as such.

The second part of the book looks at many of the key competition management issues such as scoring systems, image manipulation, and rules. Understanding the rules and the need for compliance with them is an important part of a photojudge's responsibility. We also touch on the giving of feedback and the question of disqualifications.

In the middle is a short section of visual exercises. These invite you to examine and comment on various aspects of the image. I hope those who are less experienced in talking about images will find it helpful.

Check-list for photography judges

In order to ensure you are fully comfortable when you take on the responsibilities of judging the work and photography of others (and even your own work when entering to competitions), it is useful to check your answers to these basic questions. This is a basic shopping list for your preparations. Fuller discussions of the main topics will follow:

- Are you familiar with the rules of the competition?

- If the rules are not in your first language, are you confident you understand them fully?

- Are you familiar with the competition or award aims and with the type of entries expected?

- Do you have the experience, knowledge of photography and specialist knowledge for the categories you are judging?

- Are you familiar with the scoring and marking scheme in use, and aware of their pros and cons?

- Do you have some knowledge or skill that would help you to spot fakes, plagiarised or other dubious images?

- Are you able to spot poorly executed image manipulation?

- Are you able to assess the degree and extent of image manipulation used on images using basic image manipulation tools?

- Are you able to assess the degree to which an image may be set up, arranged or posed?

- Are you up-to-date with current affairs and international news?

Basic selection strategies

ALL OF THE MANY WAYS of selecting the best or most appropriate image from a wider field of images can be reduced to two basic strategies: top-down, or bottom-up.

Each way of approaching picture selection enjoys its own strengths and weaknesses that depend, in their turn, on the purpose and context of the selection. At the same time, one may appeal more, psychologically speaking, to certain personality types than to others. So the reasons for choosing one strategy over another may be personal, and are not necessarily the worse for that.

Let's look at these approaches in more detail to assess their advantages and disadvantages.

Top-down selection

The top-down strategy aims to find the best or most promising images as quickly as possible by looking at as many images as practicable, or as many as possible at the same time. The process works by ignoring the many images that are 'maybe's' and 'possibles' in order to zero-in quickly onto the 'must have' photographs.

This strategy is needed when you have to work very quickly, as in editing for news or a sports event such as covering the Olympics or when you have large numbers of images to review quickly.

A common refinement of this strategy is to follow the first wave of selections by a further round of reviewing the non-selects or rejected photos to ensure that nothing important has been passed over.

This approach calls for a great deal of skill and experience. Depending on the subject of the photography, expertise in the subject may also be essential. For example, when editing photographs of an athletics event, editors need to know their athletics as well as being visually literate. If the sports writer needs a back rise on parallel bars, you had better not supply a picture of a basket swing, no matter how brilliant.

When judging photographs in a broader context, an excellent base in visual literacy and history of photography helps ensure a high standard of picture editing. An image that looks brilliant to an inexperienced eye could appear to an educated judge to be hackneyed, exaggerated or even clichéd. An image is more likely to impress an inexperienced or uneducated judge than one who is familiar with the whole span of photography from its inception through to contemporary movements.

As a further example, if you are judging amateur photographic competitions, it is invaluable to be familiar not only with the kind of photographs typically submitted by competitors, but also have looked at prize-winning photographs from other, similar, competitions. This is important in order to have any chance of spotting imitators, plagiarism, or even the same photograph entered into different competitions.

Advantages

- Can be very speedy for the experienced picture editor or judge.

- Possible to process a large amount of images in a short time.

- Only way to deliver usable images as speedily as possible.

- Can return to rejects for re-assessment.

Disadvantages

- May be too easy to miss the quiet, subtle or unconventional images.

Basic selection strategies

- A lot of rejects may need to be reviewed if any re-assessment is needed.

- Pressure to choose quickly can limit choice to the familiar, predictable and conventional.

- Ability to select effectively depends on high level of intense attention which lasts only a relatively short time.

- May need second or further edits - and more time - to extract the more subtle, indirect images.

- Needs large, high-resolution displays to view large numbers of thumbnail images at the same time and in good detail.

Suggestions for top-down selection

For this method to work, it's best that you assess a number of images simultaneously and in high-quality colour and high resolution. Today's large and high-resolution screens - 4K recommended, better is 8K - are ideal for the job.

With large collections of images, it is good practice to review for not longer than 45 mins at a time; better to limit to 30 mins. In practice, 50 mins on, 10 mins off is a common pattern of work and rest. (See pp.32-3 for suggestions on how to rest your eyes.)

The basic question is how large the image previews need to be for effective judgement. It's not just a matter of taste or skill level.

- **If images are very similar**, for example, sequences from a tennis match, or if the images contain a great deal of busy detail such as sequences from a street demonstration, images need to be displayed large for proper assessment. This is because the difference between a winning image and its sister can be very small - down to a minute change in expression or pose. You may need to view as few as 4 to 9 images at once and on a large screen, say, 27". A popular hybrid is to show a 'film roll' of smaller previews next to larger previews.

- **If images are quite dissimilar,** for example, from a mixed travel shoot or documentary with widely spaced events, you may be able to assess as many as 30 images on a large screen at a time. With any image management software, you can always quickly fill the screen with any image that you wish to examine more closely or use a secondary monitor for enlargements with the primary screen showing small previews.

Bottom-up selection

The bottom-up selection strategy evaluates or rates each image individually. Then you collect the highest rated images to re-evaluate them and weed out the weaker ones. You repeat the process as often needed until you reach a final selection.

The bottom-up strategy is the more methodical, more considered way to select images. If you adopt it, you will scan each image carefully - usually one at a time - and rate it either to reject or mark it as a possible 'select' entirely on its own merits. After eliminating the rejects, you repeat the process by examining the possibles and giving a score to those.

You may run another round of editing, but eventually, the best or 'must-have' image emerges from the scoring. This approach works well for small collections of images of similar quality. It is also often used where photo competition entries are scored by a panel of judges.

This approach is a safe one if you have less experience as it forces you to evaluate every image and to re-examine selected images more than once. In practice, you may very quickly spot the obvious winning images; that means that you may be combining a bit of top-down with bottom-up selection processing. That in itself is not necessarily a bad thing but it is best not to mix up different strategies as you may lose track of the status of an image.

When you gain experience, you may combine the scoring processes into one sweep. As you go through the images, you either reject it or rate it on a scale of, say, 1 to 5 points or stars. Usually, 1 star is awarded to an image that is a possible but neither is it a strong contender. 5 stars are awarded to an image that is very strong or is sure to be short-listed. The principles of scoring and issues around different systems, including whether it is better to score out of three or a hundred, will be discussed later (see from p.114).

Scoring schemes

In general, the picture selection process is binary: either the picture is selected or it is not. Systems with large scales e.g. scoring or marking between 0 -100 are suitable for competitions handling very large numbers of images with judges working independently. They are a necessity for the assessment and marking of course-work in college courses. Photographers working with their own or smaller numbers of images, or working in groups, can operate with scoring schemes with much smaller scales, such as 1 - 5.

The numbers of images awarded high marks at each stage can give a good indication of how tightly you are editing. If you end up with a majority scoring 4 or 5 stars after a first-stage edit, you can be sure that a more critical or tighter edit would be better. Of course, it may also mean that you do have a very strong collection of images in front of you!

This is a big topic that is taken up in detail in Chapter 5 p.114 and on.

Advantages

- Thorough and methodical system.

- Good way to assess overall quality of a collection if images are reviewed randomly.

- Can uncover images which would be otherwise missed.

- Can operate well with small screens e.g. laptops or tablets.

Disadvantages

- Can be very time-consuming;

- Can deliver too many options for final selection, causing further debate or need to make a further round of selections.

- Concentration on remaining selects may obscure reject errors from earlier stage or dissuade return to earlier rejects.

- Any perceived need to rank images may cause unnecessary debate.

Suggestions for bottom-up selection

This strategy works well where a number of judges or editors need to look at the same image at the same time. The image can be shown on a large screen or, better, projected to a large size. Naturally, this arrangement also makes it easy for a group of judges to debate their different views and to advance reasons to support their judgements. According to the time available and the views of the competition administration, this may or may not be regarded as a benefit.

The bottom-up strategy strategy is also a good recommendation for personal selection if you have access to only a small, low-quality screen such as a laptop or tablet. In fact, small screens may invite a more intimate, closer relationship with the image. It is a good learning tool.

As with top-down selection, if you have to deal with large collections of images, it is good practice to review for not longer than 40 - 50 mins at a time. This applies particularly if images are very similar, such as those from portrait, wedding or fashion shoots with many sister shots. In practice, 50 mins on, and 10 mins off is a common pattern of work and rest.

(See Chapter 2 pp.32-3 for suggestions on how to rest your eyes.)

Speed of review

The main practical issue here is for how much time you view an image before proceeding to the next. The issue is the speed of review. Obviously, the less time you give each image, the more quickly you can work through the queue of images. But it is not obvious that giving more time to each image improves the chances of making the correct decision every time.

- **Rapid review** - 1 to 2 seconds per image - obviously gets through a lot of images in a short time. It encourages snap decisions but requires high levels of concentration and considerable experience of judging images. The pressure to move on, and not linger can lead rapidly to fatigue and errors of judgement. In addition, the making of quick decisions tends to lead to the selection images with high and obvious impact. In contrast, the quieter, more subtle or complicated, or black-and-white images may be not be given the time needed for their fair and proper assessment.

- **Slower-paced review** - 8 seconds or more per image - is best reserved for later phases of image selection. This is because the obviously weak, clichéd or unsatisfactory images can usually be spotted in much less time - less than two seconds. If every image is given 8 or more seconds, fatigue quickly sets in if the majority of images are rejects: and long review times are really not needed.

- **Moderately paced review** - 4 to 7 seconds per image - can much increase the number of images viewed in a given time compared to slower review. This may be less tiring than rapid review, but if there are large numbers of images to be reviewed, the longer working time needed can introduce errors of judgement. In practice, this is a good average pace to keep up.

Whatever duration of review you adopt - and it's usually a matter of personal preference based on experience and skill as well as the quality of the images - the system should be flexible. It should be possible for judges to whizz rapidly through a lot of weak images, but slow down when the quality of images warrant closer attention.

Some competitions set out with a rapid pace of duration, but a 'hands up' from any judge at any time can stop the clock and allow more time for deliberation. This is a good idea in theory, but psychological and peer pressure can limit its usefulness. For example, a judge who often stops the flow of images may feel everyone getting impatient with him. Later, he may hold back from asking for a pause when it's really needed.

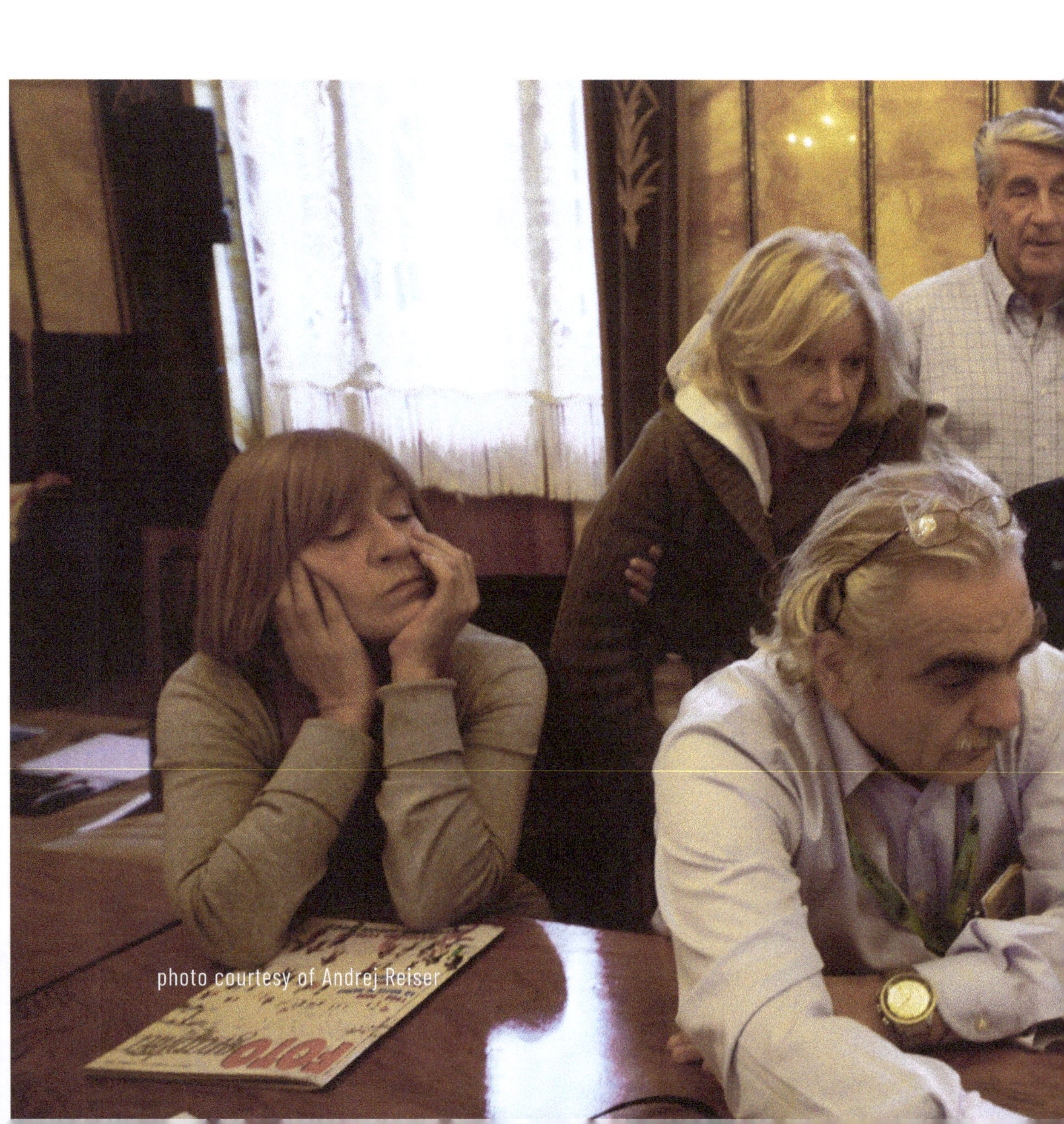
photo courtesy of Andrej Reiser

Practical matters

Chapter Two

Practical set-up

Help with fatigue

How to win with your pictures

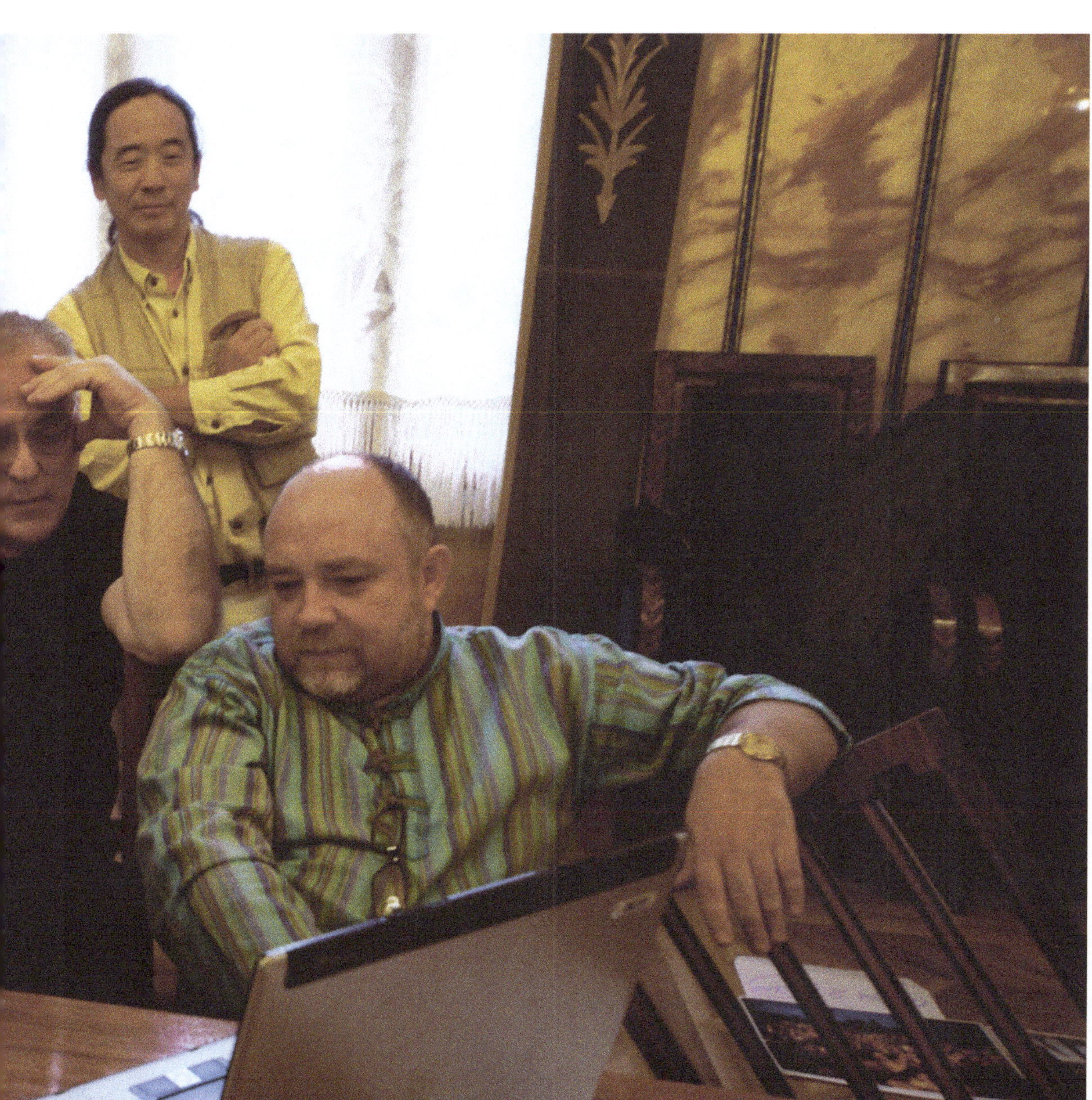

THE CARE AND HEALTH of judges' eyes should a high priority in the organisation of competition judging. But, surprisingly, this issue is often neglected. There are two main parts to the arrangements. First is the need to ensure a high quality, comfortable environment for consistent viewing. The second are measures for ensuring that judges' eyes are not strained, and to take the rests that are needed.

Viewing conditions

The most rigorous requirements for viewing prints are those operated by the printing industry for colour matching proofs. And for using monitors, the colour grading room in post-production video is also precisely defined.

In general, photo competitions do not need to meet these high standards but they should at least meet the conditions for practical appraisal as defined by the International Organisation for Standardisation.

There are five conditions which should be observed and met: colour quality, light intensity, evenness of illumination, quality of surround, and geometry of lighting. We will look at these in turn for the three different modes of viewing - print, monitor and projection.

Viewing prints

Ideally, the illumination should conform to D50: colour temperature of 5000 K, with a CRI (colour rendition index) of greater 90 i.e. it is nearly full-spectrum, like warm daylight. The brightness of the light should be around 2000 lux, not less than 1750 lux, not greater than 2250 lux. (A typical desk-lamp delivers around 1500 lux to the desk.) Evenness of illumination should be such that the darkest area is at least 60% of the brightness of the brightest part.

The surround for viewing the print should be neutral, preferably neither white nor black but a middle grey. Finally, lighting should be set up to ensure no reflections of the lights or other bright sources - such as windows - can be seen in the print.

Industry standard viewing conditions

One standard defining for industry conditions for viewing colour prints is ISO 3664-2009. The full standard can be purchased on this webpage: www.iso.org/standard/43234.html. Broadly, the standard calls for lighting that is similar to warm daylight, evenly spread, neither too bright nor too dark.

In technical summary ISO 3664-2009 requires:

- The chromaticity coordinates of a light source should be within a 0.005 radius of the D50 chromaticity coordinates.

- The colour temperature of a light source should be similar to natural daylight with a colour temperature of about 5000K.

- The relative spectral power distribution of a light source should be as close to CIE illuminant D50 as possible.

- The colour rendering index of a light source can ensure its accuracy to D50 i.e. 90 or greater. The CRI value of colour samples used to measure general CRI should be at least 80.

- The metamerism index (MI) should be less than 1.5 (not 4 as in the 2000 standard therefor it calls for more UV light than before).

Practical set up

- Consistent, steady light intensity should allow assessment of shadow detail without clipped or washed out highlights. An intensity of 500 lux is the minimum acceptable level.

- Illuminance should be even throughout the viewing area: all points should be 60% of maximum intensity at all points.

- A neutral grey i.e. not tinted, and matte i.e. not glossy surround with luminous reflectance of between 10% and 60% is specified for viewing prints.

- Light-source, subject and observer should be positioned to minimise specular reflections and glare as these are highly distracting and interfere seriously with proper print assessment.

I have personally never come across ideal viewing conditions except when working in off-set printing works, and certainly not for competition judging. This does not invalidate the judging, but the standards are perfectly well defined and competition organisers should make best their endeavours to comply with the standards to make judging as fair as possible. The most frequent failings are insufficiently bright lighting, uneven lighting and reflections on prints.

Viewing on monitors

A basic requirement of judging images on monitors is that all monitors have been calibrated and profiled so that any image viewed on any monitor will look the same on another monitor.

The differences may be small, but a colour-critical judge using an incorrectly set up monitor may give consistently poor marks, which would be unfair to the photographers.

The most widely accepted chromaticity (white

point) for monitors is D65 (approximating to cool daylight of 6500 K) but this may be regarded as too cool (blue) given that many photographers correct their images using monitors with a white point of D58 or thereabouts. The brightness of the screen should be between 150-250 candelas per square metre (cd/sqm): some authorities recommend 120 cd/sqm. On modern flat-panel displays, evenness of illumination is excellent but colours should also be even across the screen, and colours should change as little as possible when the monitor is viewed at a slight angle.

The colour space enclosed by the monitor should be at least 85% of Adobe RGB, and, of course, preferably as close to 100% as possible i.e. to show as wide a gamut of colours as possible.

Unlike the viewing of prints, the distance for viewing monitors is usually more or less set by the width of the desk, or position of the chair. TV production recommends that HD images of 1920 pixels wide should be viewed at a distance of about 3 x screen height.

Naturally, reflections on the screen should be absent for judging purposes - which means working in low-level lighting, but not in a fully darkened room. This is because in a darkened room, the frequent and often big variations in picture brightness cause large fluctuations in the viewers' pupils which in turn causes eye-strain and fatigue.

But if you locate ambient lighting behind the monitor to light the wall behind, this 'bias lighting' reduces changes in the size of the judges' pupils as they respond by taking account both the image and the bias lighting. The ambient lighting should be D65 and the background should be a neutral grey.

One widely used standard for assessing monitor quality is ITU-R BT.710-4 "Subjective Assessment Methods For Image Quality In High-Definition Television".

Viewing with a projector

Projectors, like monitors, should be calibrated and profiled based on native settings for white point and brightness, with a Gamma of 2.2 using a hardware colour calibration system.

During calibration, small adjustments may be needed in response to local conditions such as the colour of the walls and curtains of the room (that should at any rate be neutral) and the presence of a tint or colour on the projector screen itself that may range from cool white to warm white.

The projector should deliver images of HD quality (1920 pixels wide) but preferably better, deliver at least 2000 lumens of white light and offer a good (not necessarily the highest) contrast ratio. Viewing and judging of the images should take place in low ambient light, with no bright spots such as from a hole in the room's curtains or desk lamps.

The image should be key-stone corrected so that it looks undistorted to the judges. A high-quality projection screen should be used, with around 1:1 gain (i.e. not too reflective) positioned so that all judges may view the images without obstruction and from as straight-on as possible.

Unlike movies, it is permissible for the image to be slightly larger than can be taken in by the whole eye. This means the screen subtends to the eye an angle of 35° or a little more (e.g. judges should sit around 3m away from an image measuring 70" (1.8m) on the diagonal).

When transitioning from one image to another, use a fairly rapid cross-fade (lasting 0.5 sec - 1.5 sec): the first image darkens while the second becomes brighter. This is less tiring than quick or snap cuts: the first image is immediately replaced for the next. Do not use more elaborate transitions. Do not allow dark intervals between images as the constant adjustment of pupils quickly tires the eyes of judges.

Colour standardisation

Purely visual methods are not accurate enough to ensure reliable, repeatable and standardised viewing conditions. Hardware colorimeters are the most reliable and accurate way to assess viewing conditions. Ambient lighting, projector lighting, monitor screen are all different forms of lighting and call for different measurement methods. Some modern colorimeters can measure projector lighting as well as monitor screens, but may not be able to deal with ambient lighting.

Colour standardisations call for two steps of measurement. First, the light source should be calibrated i.e. measured and adjusted to ensure it meets specifications i.e. it is as bright as specified and producing a steady output (for example, it is not warming up which offers changing colour temperatures).

Once calibrated, the source is ready to be characterised: its colour characteristics can be measured e.g. whether it tends to be a little green in the shadows but yellow in the high values. This ensures that it is not only up to specification, but also provides the information for any adjustments to be made. For example, with a monitor screen or projector, the chlaracteristation defines a profile. This profile would, for example, reduce the green at low levels, and increase blue and green at high values to reduce the yellow bias.

It has to be said that while modern equipment is often well adjusted straight out of the box, it's best not to assume every item works to specifications.

Help with fatigue

Physical fatigue

Fatigue of various kinds will affect the quality of our picture judging. If you have ever wondered where a picture came from: you're sure you haven't seen it before. Then you know what happens when you're fatigued. You thought you were looking but you had literally blinked and missed it. You think you've checked an image, but in fact your eye simply slid over it. To reduce fatigue of various sorts, it will help to keep the following in mind:

- Check that your viewing conditions are as comfortable as possible.

- **Mix keyboard and mouse control**, particularly when scrolling, to reduce risk of repetitive strain injury. That is, use the up/down arrow keys for a time, then use the scroll wheel on the mouse for a time. Swap over from time to time. Use an ergonomic mouse i.e. designed to keep your wrist at a natural position.

- **Use an application that interrupts your work regularly** to force you to take a rest: the work interval generally recommended is 20 minutes between short rests of around 10 seconds, then 60 minutes between longer main rests of at least 10 minutes. There are many such apps that are free to download.

- During the main rest period, walk around, in fresh air if possible. Walk up and down one flight of stairs.

- **Rest your eyes.** Close your eyes lightly, and keep them closed for at least two minutes. You can cup your palms over your eyes, lean your elbows on the desk. Then gently rest your head in your hands. Relax your shoulders. Ideally, place a low cushion on the desk and lean on that to keep your head more upright. Save your eyes; they are the only ones you have.

- **Exercise your eyes.** Staring at a computer screen is the eye's equivalent of sitting still too long. Try this: Keeping your eyes open and head in one position look up at the ceiling straight above your head. Hold for a two seconds. Then look down as if looking down your nose. Then look to the far left. Keep these eye movements steady. Then look to your far right, as before, just by moving your eyes. Hold for a few seconds in each position.

Psychological fatigue

Another kind of fatigue is psychological in nature: it is caused by factors such as having to make a series of numerous finely tuned decisions at speed while evaluating a large number of criteria. It's hard work for the brain. Such fatigue can cause you to become confused about what you're doing and doubt your earlier decisions. So you go back over earlier rejects or re-examine your selects. You compare them with other pictures. You spend a lot of time going backwards and forwards. The deadline looms, and you push yourself harder, increasing the chances of making bad calls. Too many of us have been through this agony.

The basic pointers are:

- Give yourself regular physical breaks.

- Edit in groups of similar subjects: every shoot can be divided into smaller groups of images.

- Perform as many tasks using the keyboard rather than use the mouse or trackpad: it's much less effort

- Play calm background audio tracks designed for study, or creativity: hundreds are freely available for free download or playing online.

How to win with your pictures

ONE OF THE GREAT THRILLS for any photographer is to see your pictures published. But winning a prize with your image easily tops that. Your image has caught the eyes of the very expert (and pretty hard-to-please, firm-jawed) judges. That's rewarding in itself. But you know too that your picture has been singled out of thousands of other entries: this surely is nectar to the ego.

This section is written to help photographers see the process from the judges' point of view by sketching strategies for grabbing their attention. This is essentially a practical primer for photographers keen to win prizes or awards with photographs.

Primarily, of course, prize-winning images are fabulous shots. But you've probably looked at some winners and wondered why they won. It's because there's more to it - as you will see in the rest of the book. Here I share with you some practical applications of the points dealt with in more detail elsewhere in the book.

Go different

The world is getting smaller, we are all travelling more and to places once regarded inaccessible to all but the best-equipped expeditions. Yet the same old locations or types of locations turn up again and again in competition entries. Monasteries in Bhutan. The Taj Mahal. Canyon de Chelly. Ngorongoro Crater. Of course that's because those locations are fabulously wonderful for photography. They are, dare I say it, almost too easy to photograph.

The beauty of photograph is its ability to open your eyes. And when you open your eyes to beauties and loveliness near you, another miracle happens: you open other people's eyes too. A fine example of that is Bruce Davidson's work on Central Park, New York - not many people's first choice for a photography expedition. There is a also Josef Sudek's lifetime's observation in and around his garden shed, in all weathers and lighting. Or check out Don McCullin's still life studies made around his home.

Anyway, all too often, what happens is that competitions receive numerous images from the same place. This makes judges a little bored, they get a little testy. After looking at hundreds of images, they like to be surprised. So, if you do find yourself in one of these popular places ...

Shoot different

Try being different: look at how others photograph the famous sights and see if you can do something out of the ordinary. That's one way to surprise judges. A slant on the subject that's unusual, a funny angle, or touch of humour can work wonders to a hackneyed or clichéd location.

We have so many wonderful pictures of well-known subjects, we are at the point that the less-obvious becomes the more-noticeable. We know what elephants look like now - roaming the plains, charging at each other, charging at the cameraman, feeding on trees. So now quite an abstract shot of an elephant can make it to the top. In fact it is the very familiarity of elephant image that enables an abstract image to be easily identified. Indeed, that may now be the only kind of elephant shot that will not be passed over by judges.

This example shows that the notion of what is award-winning and exceptional will change in time.

Avoid imitating last year's winners

It's useful to learn from past winners but that's not the same as sending in a very similar shot for next year's competition. The reason is that, even if your shot is better than last year's, judges will remember;

competition administrators will remember. And no-one wants two similar-looking shots to win the top slots two years running. Or even if a year or more separates the winners.

You can imagine what photography magazines and websites, whose editors have similarly long memories, will think when they receive a picture that looks the same as a previous winner. It will not seem like new material (it's not).

For competitions that have been running a few years, it's worth looking at the past winners so you can work out what not to submit. I guess it's advice similar to previous point, but in bucket loads.

Here are some general pointers to help you succeed in competitions.

Remember the competition

You'd be amazed at how little attention people pay to the competition rules (see from p.140 for details on rules). It's obvious really, but I have to say it, having judged competitions where literally hundreds of entries have been rejected simply because they did not comply with rules in one way or another. Read the rules, follow the instructions to the letter! Let me say it again: Read the rules, follow the instructions to the letter!

In one small competition I judged, only one of the set of finalists had actually followed the rules to the letter. Strictly, we should simply have disqualified all the others. As it turned out, the only finalist who followed the rules had also submitted the best photos. Perhaps there's a lesson in that.

Technical quality tops

It also goes without saying that the technical quality of what you send in should be tops. By that I don't mean that you have to use the big shooters from Sony, Nikon, Canon, Hasselblad to make the shot as even the most prestigious competitions will accept images from 6-megapixel cameras.

But your images do have to look as if the photographer is in complete control of every step of its creation and any subsequent processing. If it's meant to be blurred, it should be blurred by just the right amount - not too much, not too little. . If the horizon is on a slant, it should convincingly so, enough to make it look deliberate. If anything is not focussed perfectly, it should be for a reason that convincingly enhances the visual message. In short, the flaw should be flawless; it does not draw attention to itself, but is integral to the image content.

And, finally, do not over-process your images. Avoid over-sharpening your images - with modern cameras and lenses it should not be necessary to add much, if any, sharpening. If you find you have to, then it's worth looking at the quality of your focusing or capture technique.

Further, it should not be necessary to pump up colours by much, if any i.e. avoid over-saturation or over-rich colours. While some kinds of image manipulation treatment come in fashion, such as heavy tone-mapping HDR (High Dynamic Range)-type treatments, they can fall out of fashion equally quickly. Compositing images with fantastic juxtapositions used to be all the rage, but they have rightly been left out to pasture. Unfortunately, none of these fashionable techniques will post you a warning in advance of their fall from favour.

In addition, be aware that judges are human, and may be more or less swayed by their pet hates. For example, some dislike images that have been turned up-side down e.g. to turn reflections upright while many find that an acceptable change. Others will make faces when they see blocked highlights or shadows or mixed white balance whereas some judges will accept these 'faults'. Moderation in image manipulation is a good policy.

Send in good time

Being human, we all have a tendency to leave things to the last minute. In the days of snail mail, that did not cause too much of a problem: the poor competition office simply got flooded with sacks of mail in the last few days to the deadline. These days, there's a real problem: when everyone tries to download images to the competition in the remaining day or two, the computer server is drowned. It can't handle the large number of simultaneous calls and its band-width - think of a canal carrying water - cannot cope with the amount being sent in all at once. It can crash like a canal flooding with rainwater. As a result files may get lost or corrupted. You may have to send again. It's stress and chaos you can do without, easily avoided by submitting in good time.

Read the sub-text

The rules for larger competitions are often long and complicated. You may find it's best to print the rules out and carry them around with you for a while. If you're not used to reading legal language, it may be very hard to take in the meaning.

Furthermore, few if any competition organisers quite get every nuance and detail of what they are wanting to put into their rules. You may have to read the sub-text or between the lines. Look at what kind of company is the main sponsor, as that could affect the choice of one of the winners.

For example if the competition is about animals, ensure that you do no stress your animal in making the photograph or use any cruel method - like tying them to one position or use live bait - to obtain your results. This may not be explicitly forbidden but you can be sure the judges will be expert at spotting the signs of such suspect practices. However, if one of the main camera manufacturers is involved, don't worry that they'll be prejudiced against shots made on other cameras (unless the rules specifically forbid it, of course). In my experience, camera manufacturers sponsor competitions in order to encourage photography in general, and are therefore broad-minded about competing camera marques.

Good luck

And here's the final ingredient. It helps to have a bit of luck. That seems to be undeniable, if perhaps a bit circular in logic. But if that's true, then the more competitions you enter, the more luck you'll have. Keep an eye open for competitions: sometimes you get the best chance when a competition is young and not attracting vast numbers of entries.

At any rate, the only guarantee is that if you don't enter, you certainly won't win.

By the way, when you search for competitions to enter, don't forget to try looking 'call for entries' in addition to the obvious search strings like 'photo competition', 'photo award' or 'photo prize'. There are many portals and compilations on the Web for you to check out.

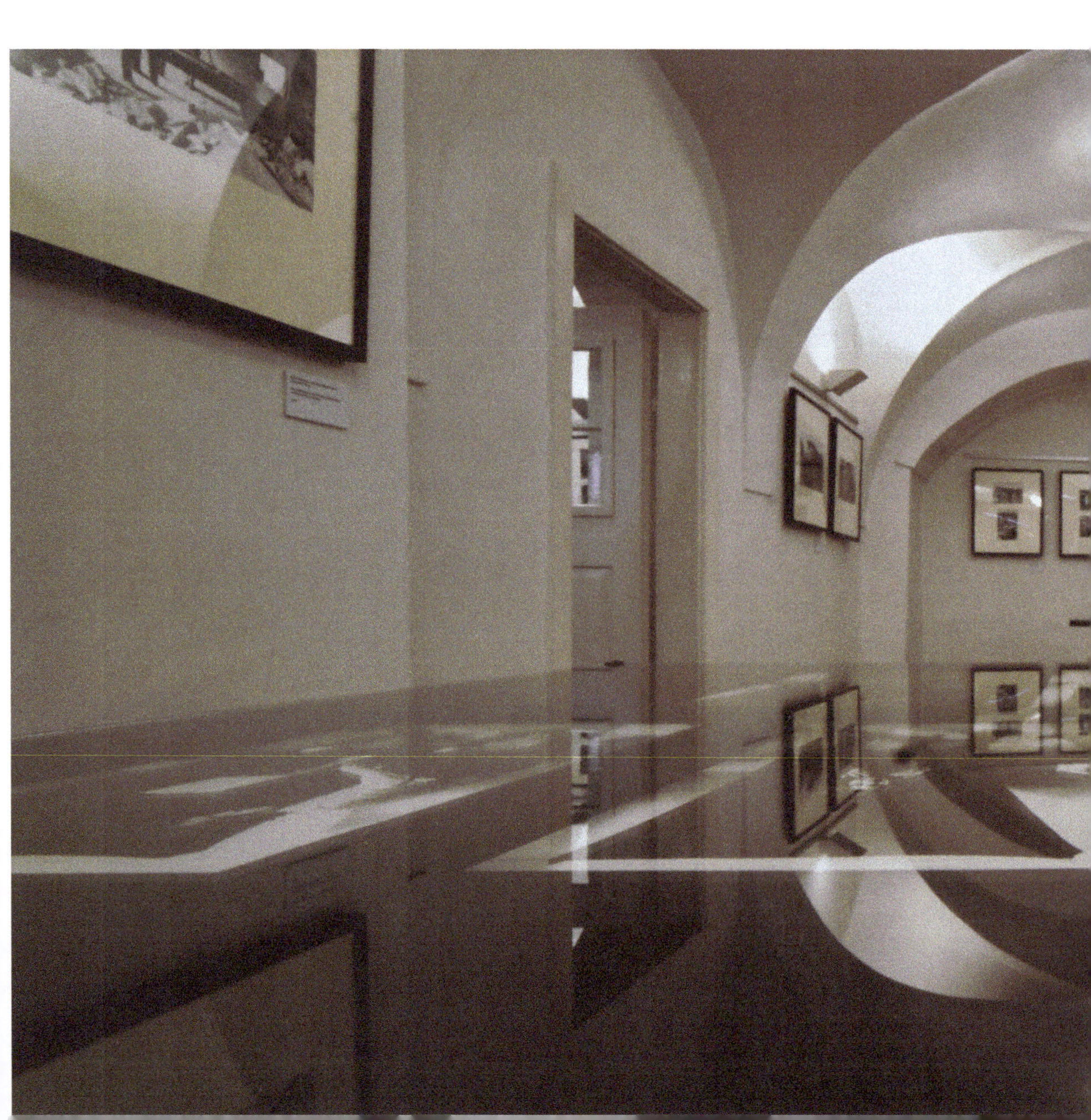

General concepts

Chapter Three

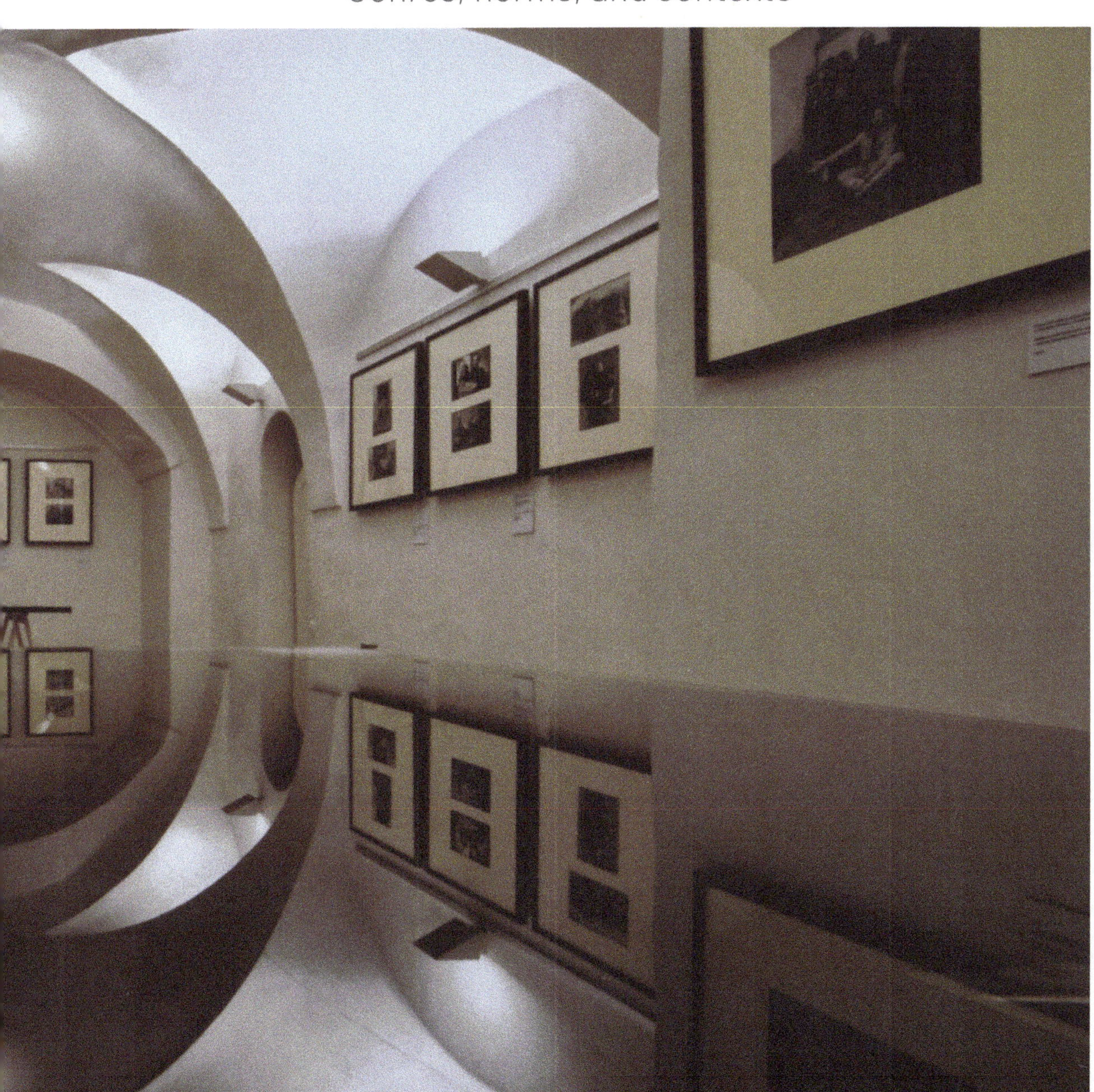

Levels of appreciation

WHEN YOU LOOK AT A PHOTOGRAPH, many very complicated things happen, sometimes all at once. You may instantly recognise the subject of the photograph. You may notice whether it is in black and white or in colour. You may recognise that it is a classic photograph that you've seen many times, or decide it's one that you've never seen before. Other issues, such as whether the photographer acted appropriately may come to mind too.

The five levels of appreciation

For the large majority of purposes, you don't need to analyse the ways in which different factors affect your assessment of the image. Also, for most non-photographers and even photographers, it is not important to understand how exactly you arrive at an opinion about a picture.

But if you are judging the work of others, if your decisions can launch a photographer's career, then the bases or reasons for your judgement of a photograph become very important.

Here, we will look at the five steps or levels of appreciation that most people grow through in the process of image assessment. They rise in complexity from what can be read by a machine, to an appreciation that requires a great deal of visual experience, and training. The progression also rises from the nearly instinctual through conscious thought to a complex of critical modes.

1   Basic content

At the most basic level, the image is simply information that depicts something. At this level, what the image shows can be 'read' by machines - whether it's showing a car number plate, an =industrial component or blood cells. Analysis of the digital image is not of the image as we see it, but as a matrix, or a sequence of numbers. Artificial intelligence based on deep learning can achieve results similar to basic human identification of images but the basic data level remains what: the things that the photo shows, what it's of - whether it's a cat or a building.

Even at this basic level, images may be rejected for a competition. This is simply because it is of something that is not permitted: a domestic dog entered for a wildlife photography competition, a portrait photo entered in the still-life section, and so on. The job of the first filter judging (see p.115) is usually to eliminate images which do not comply with the rules at this level.

2   Technical

The technical assessment of an image can also be undertaken largely by machines. Instruments can assess colour or white balance, colour saturation, overall sharpness, dynamic range and tone quality through image processing algorithms. In fact, image manipulation applications do this all the time. The displays of colour values, levels histograms are essentially software analyses of the image data.

Visually, most photographers can make the same assessments, although on a less reliable, less precise basis. Beginner photographers may not have the same skills as experienced photographers to assess factors such as white balance or sharpness. But you can improve these skills with practice. The point is that human assessment of technical aspects of the image are subjective in quality while having an objective basis. This means we can always check or back up our visual assessment by making a technical measurement.

Keep in mind, however, that different software applications may use different ways or settings to calculate complicated measures such as white balance. As a result, they may render the same image in somewhat different ways. This means that even software can be a little 'subjective' in their assessment of an image.

As you know, technical and physical assessments of an image are fundamental in judging photographs in competitions. We discuss this in great detail in the Chapter 4 Technical dimensions (from p.68).

3 Cultural/Aesthetic

The next level of appreciation builds on the basic levels of identifying the subject of the photograph - what it is showing - and the technical features of the image. This next level assesses how interesting, attention-grabbing, or moving we find the picture. We apply terms like 'beautiful', 'stunning' in the case of approval and 'dull', 'boring', 'ordinary' when we aren't impressed.

Normally, this appreciation happens quickly for the modern viewer because most of us have a great deal of practice in judging photos. A typical urban dweller sees over 2000 images each day as they walk along streets, sit in buses, walk past window displays, skim through newspapers. With ready access to social media and picture-sharing sites, people could easily view even more images in a day.

We may ignore almost all, but you know that you're constantly scanning and judging every image because, from time to time, you will turn to look more closely at one photo. A new film featuring your favourite actor, special bargains at your local store, a stunning landscape showing a holiday destination that you have been dreaming about.

At this level, we leave most image analysis algorithms far behind. We bring a vastly rich and complicated weave of personal histories, interests and preferences, cultural influences and learnt responses to our evaluation of images.

Nonetheless, the overall reaction is fairly summary and superficial in character. We ignore, or we like but move on, or we may pause for a second look. At this level, there is no clear separation between our response to the image itself - its aesthetic qualities and its subject matter - with our feelings about the subject itself. For example, we pay attention to a portrait not because it's a great image but because it shows our favourite actor. Or someone may look at a photo of a car just because it shows something that he wishes he could afford. In large measure, the assessment is not conscious. Nor is it the result of considered thought, but made up of mostly sub-conscious, or sub-liminal emotional responses.

The majority of responses to images by inexperienced judges, or experienced viewers not paying too much attention, operate at this level.

4   Critical evaluation

At this next level, we apply conscious thought and evaluation to the immediate feelings or emotions aroused by an image. This is the level of assessment of an image that we commonly associate with judging images. We ask ourselves what it is about the image that appeals to us, or analyse how it achieves its impact or conveys its meaning.

This is the stage at which we examine the image, as well as interrogate our own response to it.

We may also look with forensic intentions. We are alert for signs of image manipulation that may be illegal under the rules. We may search for signs that an image that purports to be of a news or wildlife event may, in fact, have been staged. We look outside the frame, as it were - even behind the image - as part of our search for clues.

This level of assessment takes place in a fully conscious mind that is carefully directed. It is usually easily articulated and expressed in words compared to the reaction at earlier levels which are likely more visceral and sub-conscious. You may feel that this evaluation is too negative in that it is critical. It actually sets out to look for trouble in one form or other. It is an assessment, an appraisal. We look for infractions of rules; we look for reasons to lower the score.

Put in more positive way, at this stage, the photojudge wants to be forced to promote the image - to be given an award, or selected for exhibition. And the photographer is hoping the picture is so convincingly excellent, it resists all attempts to find fault with it.

5   Sequential relationships

At the previous levels of assessment, we look at only the single image, and we assess it essentially in isolation. It is true we bring our experience and knowledge of other images we have seen in the past. We may also bring in side factors such as the rules of a competition, the requirements of a publisher or curator. We may consider even quite exterior factors such as religious and legal limits to the photographs we can use. For all that, our attention focuses on the single, solitary image.

The next higher level of evaluation is more specialised and, generally, the only people who are concerned with it are book designers, exhibition curators, magazine editors as well as photojudges. At this level, we evaluate an image in the context of a sequence of several related others. Many competitions, award and certification schemes ask for images to be presented in a panel consisting of a group of, say, at least five images. Judges look at these images as a set or a group, and also individually. They examine how well the adjacent images relate to each other as well as how each image relates to the whole set and whether the set as a whole makes a coherent visual statement.

In a similar way, designers and exhibition curators will create a sequence of images that flow from one to another to create a coherent narrative. This evaluation assesses images not only in themselves, but in the way they relate to their near and distant neighbours, how they promote the overall story. This process involves a complicated mesh of perceptual processes, and is highly determined by culture norms. For example, while in Western societies it is natural to read a sequence of images from left to right, in Middle and Far East societies many viewers would feel more natural reading from right to left. This is, technically a meta-assessment of an image in that it uses individual images as the building blocks for new level of assessment. The result of a meta-assessment is that an image that, in itself, may not be of the highest calibre could be essential to the success of a sequence of images.

We will look at this level of assessment in detail in Chapter 4: Panel sequencing, from p.98.

Photographic ethics

PHOTOGRAPHY JUDGES ARE ESSENTIALLY gatekeepers. The vast majority of images enter a crowded place marked "Not Selected". A rare few nervously shuffle past the gate marked " Winners". That's because the great majority of images offer few reasons - if any - to be selected, but many reasons to be rejected.

One of the reasons for rejecting an image is unlike any other kind of image judgement because it doesn't refer to the photographic or visual qualities of the image. Instead, it examines actions the photographer took to obtain the image. It may also take account of the circumstances around the photography. If the actions are judged unacceptable or reprehensible in some way, the photograph may be rejected, and this can take place however wonderful its visual qualities. These considerations are based on ethical and moral issues.

Ethics and morals

These terms are often used interchangeably, but they do mean different things and it's worth keeping them distinct. Ethics is the theory, while morals are the practical application of the theory. For example, a commonly accepted moral rule is that it is wrong to tell lies. People from different societies, religions and cultures may all agree on the vital importance of that rule. But different people arrive at it from different ethical foundations. Some may believe that it is wrong to lie because that is what their religion teaches. Others use arguments based on what they consider is needed for society to work efficiently.

In photography, and photographic judging in particular, ethical thinking derives from the notion that the greater good is more important than individual gain, or personal advantage. This means that we try to act in ways that benefit everyone now and in the future. And we avoid doing things that harm anyone, any beings or damage the future. in some way For example, it does not take elaborate ethical argument to find that presenting someone else's work as your own is not a good thing to do, that it is wrong, whatever short-term benefit might be gained.

Ethics in photography

Ethical issues oversee your every photographic action. To the extent that ethics matters to you, it is continually in the background to judgements you make about any photograph. This is true whether you are a fresh beginner or a veteran professional. It doesn't matter whether you photograph food or famine, war or wilderness, whether your commissions lead you to babies or to buildings. Even if you photograph only for your own pleasure, and never show your images to anyone, photographic ethics will sooner or later become a concern of yours whenever your actions involve someone or something else.

Ethics matters to all photographers for roughly the same reason as ethics matters to you as an ordinary person. You prefer to do right instead of wrong. You would rather do good things than cause bad things. You don't wish to harm others, and don't like it if others hurt you. And, if you're working as a professional, you will care that photographers and photography is held in high regard in society.

Ethics in judging

Much of the time we take it for granted that photographers are fairly sound in their ethics, and behave in broadly moral ways. After all, we can't go around spelling out every single rule that applies to every bit of behaviour. As a result, the majority of photography competitions are not explicit about the ethical standards they expect from a photographer.

Only in two genres is it common for the need for ethical behaviour to be stated clearly. One, as you would expect, is photojournalism and news photography. The other is wildlife and animal photography.

Where a competition explicitly forbids certain actions, one of the jobs of a judge is clear enough. It is to ensure no winning image breaks the rules. For example, a wildlife photography competition may forbid use of live baiting to lure animals within camera range. As a judge you will be on the lookout for signs of unusual behaviour in the animals that may signal the use of bait (from the obvious such as half a salmon caught by an osprey to the less obvious like a domestic goat caught by a leopard). Or, taking photojournalism as an example, judges would be expected to look out for examples of artificially posed or set-up shots, inaccurate captioning or excessive use of image manipulation.

Where judges apply rules set by the competition, one could argue that they are not making any judgements based on their personal ethics and morals but are simply applying the rules. Nonetheless it is important to recognise that certain rules are motivated by a concern to uphold and promote ethical and morally sound behaviour. Examples include rules that forbid harm being done to animals being photographed, or those that forbid the removal of any details in an image, however inconsequential they may appear.

Moral behaviour in photography

Where competition rules have nothing to say about how photographers should conduct themselves before or after photography - and that is the large majority - photojudges may still be expected to exercise their moral judgement. In some situations, even in the absence of relevant rules, a judge may feel compelled to consider the morality of a photographer's actions. This usually happens when there are visual clues in the image which alert a judge to something suspicious about the image. Much depends on expert knowledge held by the judges, as well as a sensitivity to internal clues in the image as opposed to simply assessing its visual or aesthetic equalities. A wide general knowledge of current affairs is also a big advantage. Most important is whether the judge directs attention to spotting problems. Naturally, detailed interrogation of an image is pointless with anything but images being considered for a prize or award.

- A judge may know that **cultural norms** would make it all but impossible to photograph a scene in a certain country in exactly the way the photographer claims. For example: the claims of a male photographer to have obtained informal, candid images of intimate moments of young female living in a strict Muslim country deserve close scrutiny.

- A judge may be familiar with a location and know that the **caption information** is, at best inaccurate, or worse. deliberately misleading. For example, in order to complete a set of images about a certain town, an image from a different town has been slipped in. Or that a photograph that claims to be of wild birds in fact features semi-domesticated birds responding to feeding (I known it happen that they were familiar to one of the judges). This could be regarded as live baiting, contravening a rule.

- A judge may suspect that in order to obtain a certain perspective on a famous landmark, the photographer had to have taken **illegal steps** to enter a prohibited area or they may have put themselves at risk of injury. To award such an image may have the effect of encouraging more of the same illegal or dangerous behaviour.

These examples may seem too hypothetical or perhaps too far-fetched to be taken seriously. In fact all are taken from true-life examples, some of which I was personally involved in as a judge.

The point of taking such issues seriously is that the reputation of the competition and that of the organisers, judges and even sponsors, are on the line as they are wide open to public scrutiny. More, the reputation of photography and photographers may also be at stake. All of these concerns are part of the responsibility not only of photography judges but of all photographers.

That is why, if suspicions turn out to be well founded, we can expect serious consequences for the photographer to follow. These could include disqualification or a warning, depending on how the competition organiser wishes to proceed.

Wider responsibilities

If you suspect that some of these discussions may turn out to be controversial, and decisions even more so, you're correct. For some, making decisions about the rights and wrongs of a photographer's actions is already to over-extend the notion of judging photography. But there is more.

Depending on personal beliefs, or moral sensitivity, you might think there are other issues that relate to the right and wrong ways to photograph or behave as a photographer.

If, as a judge, you suspect that a photographer has taken morally dubious steps to obtain a photograph, whatever you then choose to do reflects on your moral position. For example, suppose a photographer says that his image depicts an under-aged girl being exploited in prostitution ring. Judges need to consider very carefully the implications of awarding the image a prize, bearing in mind that any award-winning image will be widely publicised.

Moral issues are not just about subject exploitation where the moral issues may be fairly clear-cut. A softer edged problem is one of authenticity. The question here is not so much about whether the image truly depicts what the photographer saw, but the genuineness of what was presented to be photographed. For example, it is now common for workshops to be arranged with models, props and lighting all carefully set up so that a photographer only needs to focus and release the shutter. Do such images qualify as the work of the photographer?

Another example is the 'historical' theme park that assembles picturesque characters dressed in ancient clothes and located in photogenic old villages. Some of these are beautifully lit with artfully smoky lighting to catch 'sun beams'. A photographer who wanted travel shots of characteristic old villages needs only buy an entrance ticket. Once in you don't even need to ask permission to photograph anyone as their job is to pose to be photographed. These theme parks and tourist attractions have produced major prize-winning photographs. To many - but not to everyone - the lack of authenticity of these images raises troubling ethical questions.

We return, then, to the importance of being clear about our individual position on photographic ethics, and on how we wish to discharge our responsibility for the resulting moral position. If you're judging your own work and not showing it to the public, you are broadly free to do what you like so long as your original photography did not infringe the rights of others. However, if you are judging a photographic competition or award with international dimensions, then your moral stance is a highly visible public one that reflects on the competition. In that case, when questions arise - as they increasingly do - it is wise to have had your ethical position sorted out.

Genres, norms and contexts

A PHOTOGRAPHIC GENRE is a way of classifying or grouping certain tendencies in photography. The notion of genre in photography refers to arranging a class or collection of images that are identified by a certain aesthetic type, by sharing visual character, by subject matter, or by a shared ideological approach.

Just like other ways of classifying - whether we are classifying movies, or wines or animals - there are many ways to approach the task. This can be understood in several ways, such as by origins, or approach, by intended use, or by medium used. These ways may be culturally determined, so it is not safe to assume that what you understand by a certain genre will be shared by someone from a different culture or with a different history.

Placing the image in a genre influences the way the image is viewed and determines a set of norms used to judge and evaluate it. Accurate and appropriate placement - perhaps also one that is sympathetic and understanding - is a precondition for the sound judgement of photography.

Identifying genres

For the photographer, the issue of identifying a genre is important when evaluating an image for use - whether it is suited for publication in a current affairs magazine or better for a travel website. For the photography judge, identifying an image's genre may be a crucial step in arriving at a judgement, especially in competitions that are genre-specific - such as portraiture, or landscape.

By and large, photo competitions define their own genres, so the majority of entries are consistent in genre. But within a genre may be sub-categories. For example, a competition for wedding photographers will expect only images made at weddings or around the ceremony. But within that set may be found portraits, still-life and images of small figures in a large landscape. Nonetheless judges would expect that all images denote some aspect of the ceremony.

Placing a photograph within an appropriate genre helps - and may be essential - for providing a framework for judgement. This in turn guides the norms which may be applied in assessing an image. For this to take place fully, it is usually essential to have knowledge of the context around the making of the photograph under review. This means that judging an image refers to more than what's in the picture itself, but also to its relationships to other factors such as the circumstances leading up to its capture.

If you fail to pay proper attention to these relationships, a mis-match between your expectations and those of the photographer is likely. This in turn can lead to unfair or erroneous decisions. According to its perceived genre, a photograph may find itself judged according to certain normative values or expectations. For example, the fine art world assesses images in a markedly different way from judgements made in amateur camera clubs. As a result, the art world's acclaim of an image of a potato on a black background seems inexplicable to the camera club.

Appreciating photographic genres will lay for you the groundwork for understanding how the perception of a genre impacts on our judgements. It's easy to see how different photographers arrive at different evaluations if their identification of genres are different. One is not necessarily better or worse than the other, though one may be more accurate.

Classify by subject

A genre defines itself most easily through the subject being photographed, for example, pets or new-born babies, sailing boats or racing cars. With some subjects, the scope for variety in other ways (use of special effects, expressiveness, exaggeration of, for example, pose or gesture) may be limited.

This can be limited by the nature of the subject, for example, footballers and rugby players are limited in what they can do on the pitch. Or it can be constrained by the intended use, for example, limits on photos for reporting news are very different from those used for social portraiture, or when recording milestone events such as christenings and birthdays. For these subjects, normative requirements guide and create genre-specific expectations.

There is always room for a re-definition of expectations through the strength of innovative image-making and also with changing tastes in society. With wedding photography, for example, the straight-up recording of the wedding event, with formal groups of guests were once the norm. But styles have shifted to allow fantasy portraits in exotic locations, sometimes elaborately illuminated, sometimes with exaggerated expressions and poses. Wedding photographs may no longer record the ceremony but provide a stage-set for the drama of the union. At the other extreme, a wedding may be photographed in the style of a social documentation with a fly-on-the-wall approach, with minimal posing, no artifice and only in ambient light.

Where there exists a variety of approaches within a genre, the judging of photographs is made rather more complicated than if the approach is mono-thematic. Wedding photography, with its fairly distinct sub-genres, is more tricky to evaluate than, say, wildlife photography which follows strict rules that forbid restraining, baiting, or in any way influencing the animal's behaviour. As we will see later, the understanding that you have of what is proper or not proper in a photographic genre gives rise to norms - the values to which you appeal when making judgements.

Some examples of subject categories include:

- stadium, and track sports events

- nature and wildlife

- news and documentary

- nude and 'glamour' or 'boudoir'

- fashion: from haute couture to catalogues

Classify by approach

Genres may also be defined by broad stylistic approaches to photography of a particular subject. Deciding on the genre takes cues from artistic gestures and ways of handling a subject. For example, portraits may be made in a surrealist manner - a disembodied head in an upside-down world. Or the same face could be rendered in pictorialist style, in soft-focus, with mournful expression against craggy rocks. Or again the same face could be rendered with modernist minimalism, lit flat against a white background, all attention on the eyes, mouth and expression.

Naturally, within each genre, you can expect to see many different subjects: e.g. pictorialism can be applied to landscapes, still-lifes, or interior scenes. But there is a natural limit for each approach: pictorialism applied to social documentary sounds like an oxymoron (not totally, but almost). And while posed bodies and faces can be expected in surrealist photography, in news photography, such setting up of the image would be a travesty or, at best, a practice of dubious authenticity.

It follows that for a given subject genre, there could be many ways to approach the photography. With social events, a photographer could work in a photojournalistic style as if she is observing and recording a news event: nothing posed, nothing directed, everything shot in natural light. Or the event may be rendered more formally, with the photographer setting up groups, posing groups, shooting with the aid of flash, carefully styling clothes for maximum smartness. Depending on a judge's tastes and local norms, some approaches may be deprecated, others praised.

Classify by art-critical status

Fine art photography allows itself a very wide range of subject matter. In fact, just about anything that can be photographed can be regarded as fine art. From fantasy portraits to still-life to large-scale tableaux arranged outside, to photography of war to landscapes and flower arrangements. The range of treatment is equally unlimited, anything from daguerreotypes, to images left to rot in the ground. All may qualify for entry.

In short, fine art photography tends not to be defined by its subject matter nor by the physical treatment of the image. The common thread that runs through all is the driving force from a conceptually motivated, art-critically aware and articulated position.

Fine art occupies itself with critical issues of cultural or social debate such as what does it mean to be representational, how text relates to image, how one's identity or political ideals mould the images one creates. In addition, if certain works of the past are admitted as art works - an agenda set by curators and museum directors - they may be also adopted into the halls of fine art photography.

In judging fine art, the artist's statement, explaining the motivations, the aims, the debate being addressed, and so on, is of much greater importance than in other genres. In fact, many photographers working in other genres would not or could not even start on the road of articulating the art-critical position that they occupy. For some competitions and awards, the artist's statement is of crucial importance to the assessment of the photographic work; it is integral to the photography itself. Indeed, it could make all the difference.

A coherently expressed and compelling statement, supported by pertinent sociological or philosophical references, can transform what looks like mundane images into a pointed comment expressed through photography.

This means that succinct cogency of expression in the competition's dialect (i.e. that of art-critical studies) may be an essential part of the photographer's skillset. By the same token, a rambling, confused statement is likely to compromise how the work is judged.

It also follows that work that may be highly regarded in one genre, may not be valued in the fine art world, and vice versa. Wildlife photography, for instance, typically makes no headway into fine art, with extremely rare exceptions. Likewise sports photographs, apart from a handful of historic images, are never admitted to fine art galleries in their own right. But portraits of sports figures may be regarded as fine art if the photographer has a reputation in fine art portraiture or if the work exploits a sports subject, such as a body-builder, to examine debates of masculinity in the feminine.

Examples of fine art genres:

- investigations of subject/text relationships

- critiques of sexual or cultural identity

- criticism of representation in photography

- representational politics of sexual identity

- post-colonisation appropriation

Influence of genre on judging

In many cases, a certain style or approach to a particular subject group is expected given an image's membership of a genre group. It is important when judging any photograph to be aware of its intended genre, whether that has been explicitly stated or only implied. The reason is that the photograph's genre provides a group of expectations that will influence your judgement.

For example, if you expect street photography to comprise candid, un-posed shots grabbed on the street, then if all the subjects appear posed in front of a backdrop, you may not accept these as street photographs even though they were made on a street. It could then be difficult to judge them against candid street photography.

Should there be a mismatch between what a judge expects to see in a photograph belonging to a certain genre and what a photographer wishes to show, then the photograph is likely to be placed at a serious disadvantage right from the start.

For example, when judging photographs in a portrait category, a judge may expect to see photographs that have been carefully lit and posed in a studio environment. If a photographer submits a portrait made in a street market at night, it might not have the refinement and clean qualities of a studio-based image. As a result, even if it is a powerful image, it could be marked down harshly. This may or may not be unjust depending on how clearly the portrait category had been defined. The justice of the decision depends on the extent to which the understanding of the photographer coincides with that of the judge regarding what is meant by the portrait genre. This is because the notional understanding of a photographic genre carries with it a set of expectations or norms to which a photographer is expected to conform. Let's discuss this now.

Norms

In general terms, norms are what you understand to be the rules from society that guide your behaviour. They are what help you to decide what you can or cannot do in a given context. When applied to photography, norms in a particular genre make up a set of notions that are supposed to tell you the acceptable or unacceptable ways to obtain your photographs. They may also mark out how far you can go with image manipulation. These norms commonly find expression in the rules of competitions relating to, for example, how images were obtained (whether setting up is permitted, for example), the extent of image manipulation that is allowed or whether captions are a material part of the submission.

Note that here that norms are not concerned with right or wrong, not with moral or ethical rules. These may all be related, but that does not affect this discussion.

Depending on the genre, the norms may be more or less explicit. In documentary and photojournalism,for instance, norms are well developed and articulated as they are needed to preserve certain core values of journalism and reporting. Similarly, in wildlife photography, there are actions - such as putting the subject at risk of abandoning its nest - which are unacceptable. In other areas - such as in advertising, fashion and photography at social functions - expectations regarding your behaviour as a photographer are neither so well defined nor so rigorous. In those genres, it is fully expected that you control and manipulate as many elements as you need to obtain the results you wish for. Subjects can be posed, asked to do improbable actions or make silly expressions, and so on.

As norms create the background against which photography operates, they may be taken for granted when competition rules are drawn up. But they are still applied during judging. For example, in some societies, exposure in any form of almost any body part is completely unacceptable. It may not be necessary to draft a rule forbidding nudity: everyone simply knows never to award a prize to any nude, irrespective of its artistic quality as an image. Nonetheless, it is possible that in every other respect it's the strongest, most striking and though-provoking image in the competition - clearly a worthy winner. For all its display of photographic skill, it will still find itself on the reject pile.

As norms often operate under the radar of explicit statement, here are a few pointers for judges to keep in mind:

- **The extent to which image manipulation is allowed varies widely.** Even within a given genre, the scope of norms is often expressed in confused ways. The limits of what is acceptable is also fluid and changes over time, and as new technologies enter the mainstream e.g. artificial intelligence image repair. For a far more detailed discussion, see Chapter 4, from p.106.

- **Religious restrictions may operate in certain countries** and if based on prevailing beliefs in the home country of the competition, it may not be explicitly stated. Images that mock or show any sign of disrespect to religious leaders or revered figures may also be automatically disqualified.

- **Images that incite racial hatred, violence, sedition, rebellion, intolerance** are likely to be - in the majority of countries - forbidden or held to be illegal. In the absence of competition rules that explicitly forbid these and similar categories, the best policy is for judges and photographers to exercise caution. It is best not to assume news, documentary or photojournalism are automatically exempt.

- **Images of children i.e. minors, whether decently attired or not, may be illegal** in any form. In some countries, the mere possession, transmission or reception of such images may be illegal. If such images are submitted to a competition, they will obviously be rejected early. In fact competition organisers may have a legal obligation to report the entry to the authorities. On the other hand, a legitimate subject for investigative documentary photography may be children who are victims of abuse or exploitation. The exercise of great care here is obligatory.

- **Certain subjects that can be freely photographed in one country may be illegal in others.** In many countries it is illegal to photograph any buildings flying the national flag, any bridges, military installations or airports. The absence of a signs prohibiting photography should be relied on to give permission to photograph. If in doubt, do not photograph.

Contexts

From this discussion flows the fact that, according to the context in which you see a photograph, you will expose it to certain predispositions when making your judgements.

For example, if you show the same photograph of a male nude in Western Europe and in the Middle East you can expect dramatically different receptions. By the same token, the same photograph of, say, a potato on a black background, may be regarded as Fine Art when judged within the institution of art galleries, yet be mocked or viewed with incredulity when viewed in camera clubs all over the world.

Genres, norms, and contexts

There is a whole history to be written on the changing reception of images relative to shifting cultural norms, the cycles of tastes, as well as the influence of institutions such as art colleges, museums or galleries as fashionable theories shape the thinking of new generations. Images judged scandalous at one time may be hailed as revolutionary; revered and shown at major galleries not many years later. Images dismissed as worthless of attention may become influential masterpieces.

The change is obviously entirely in the perception shaped by fashion. After all, the images stay exactly the same. The history of photography is piled high with examples, the most famous include Julia Margaret Cameron, Eugene Atget, Josef Sudek.

In short, the cultural and social contexts of an image regulate its reception. But contexts change fluidly and frequently, while their influence on the way we read and understand an image often changes radically over time.

For the photography judge, some points to bear in mind include:

- Be aware that the **application of rules that is too rigid** may stifle innovation and inventive work. Generally, it is preferable to be relaxed about issues based on tastes, certainly at the early stages of judging.

- If **winners of a competition will be exhibited in different countries,** certain genres of images are likely to prove more sensitive to changes in contexts and different viewerships than others. Images such as those showing nudity, violence, partially unclothed children may call for especially careful consideration.

- It is **better to make an error of judgement in favour of work that is original,** counter, innovative or challenging than in favour of work that is not shocking, surprising, or inventive.

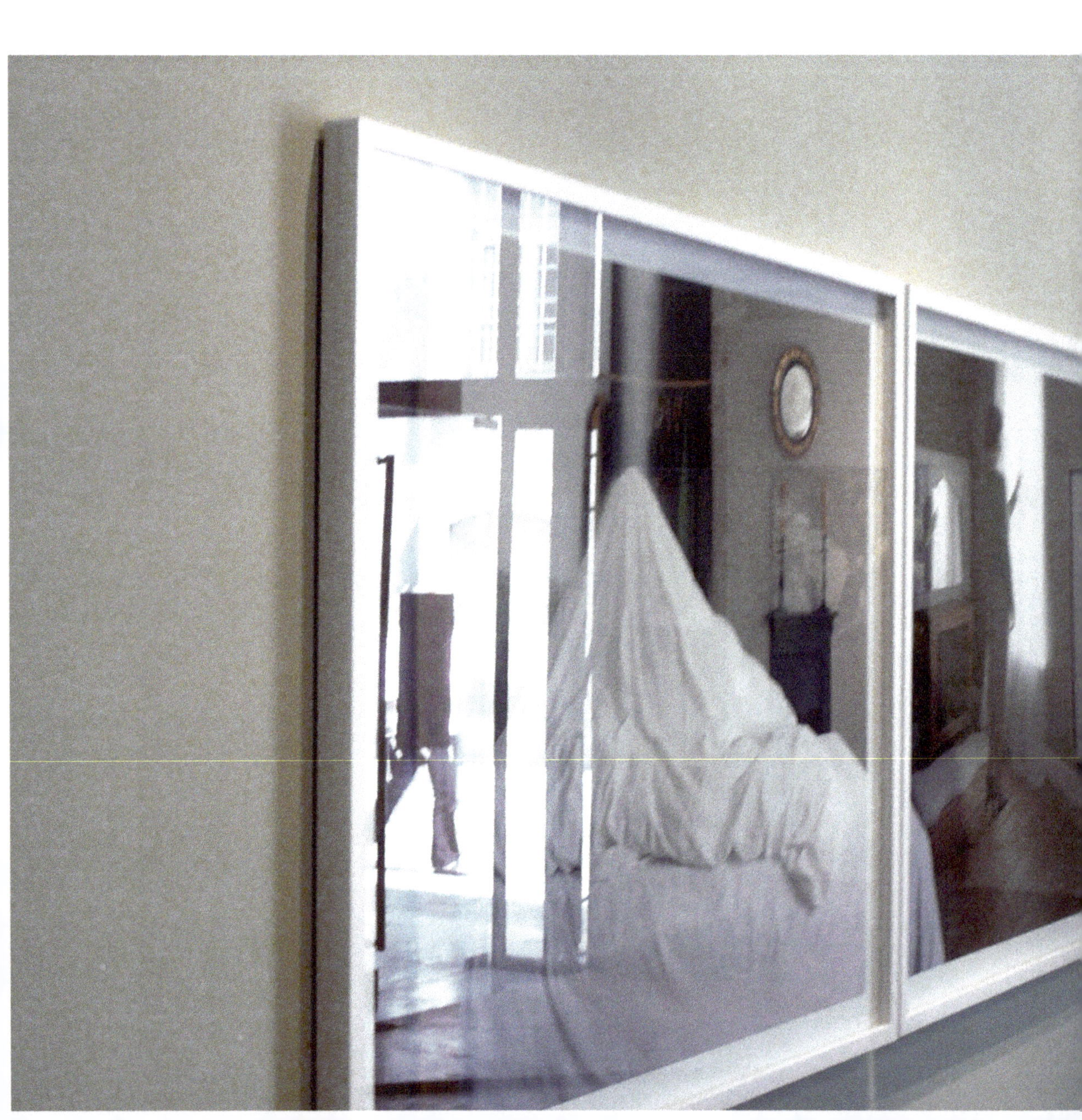

Dimensions of judging

Chapter Four

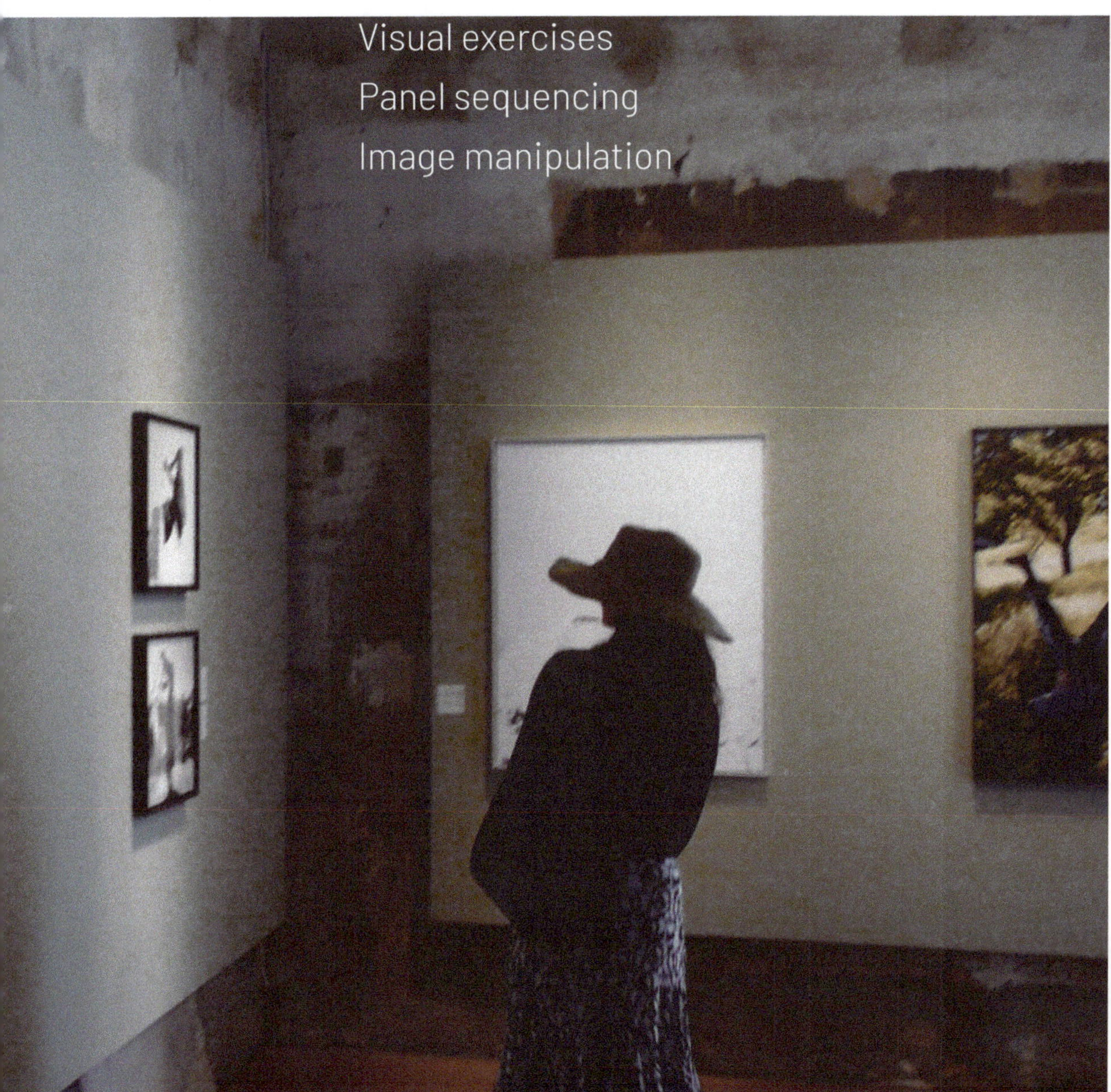

Technical dimension

THE TECHNICAL DIMENSIONS of an image describe and measure visual features that are independent of the subject depicted. Sharpness, levels, colour balance, tonality are all ways to describe an image without ever mentioning the image's subject.

Their technical nature makes them amenable to more or less objective description and precise measurement. This has put technical features in the centre of much photojudging. At the very least, all photojudging - whether in the personal context or for competitions and awards - require images to meet a certain standard of technical quality. But it can go further: in some contexts, images may be judged almost entirely on their technical merit. This difference in emphasis may carry a great deal of weight. Therefore it is important to be explicit about the importance of technical quality.

Image size

Image size counts up the number of pixels used to create the image. You will find image size quoted in pixel dimensions, for example, 3000 x 2000 pixels. Or it may be quoted in MP or megapixels - millions of pixels - such as 6 MP. It is the fundamental measure of image quality in that it sets the number of pixels used to form an image of a given quality. While the measure itself is objective, its relation to image quality is not. The minimum for a given quality depends on the intended use of the image. (By the way, this figure is generally much smaller than most photographers think.)

While image size counts up the number of pixels used to form the image, resolution measures the density of pixels used to create an output image. Formerly, image size and resolution had to be treated separately. In current practice, thanks to automatic sizing by software, images are usually automatically resized to ensure they fit the platform or device being used.

- Complying with the image size demanded by a competition is an elementary requirement which all photographers should be able to carry out. Failure to do so - even if by a seemingly insignificant amount - may automatically disqualify an entry.

File size

Competitions and grant-awarding bodies frequently set a limit on file sizes of images that can be submitted. Some will set out not only image size but also file size. This is mainly for the convenience of the organisers as the limits help manage the bandwidth or amount of data that has to be handled, particularly when hundreds of thousands of images are entered. But it is also a help to the photographer to avoid sending files larger than needed.

Note that two images with identical pixel dimensions (i.e. the same image size) and the same compression ratio may differ in file size according to the amount of detail that needs to be compressed. Images with more fine detail e.g. an intricately detailed nature shot will compress to a larger file than one with large areas of even tone e.g. a seascape with even skies.

- Many websites for competition and awards automatically refuse to accept files that are larger than the set limit. Competition organisers can ask their web engineers to reject files that are too large.

- Today's cameras enable photographer to create files that are much larger than those needed for competition judging, but minimum file sizes should be set if the competition wishes to make exhibition prints or to publish a book of winning images.

Image levels

Correct exposure is one of the fundamental requirements of the image. This does not mean that overall, the image levels must always average out or integrate to mid-tone grey. Low-key images are supposed to look dark, and show a corresponding Levels display (histogram) that is weighted to the left. Equally, high-key images are supposed to look light with histogram peaks shunted to the right.

In short, we expect to see an image exposed in a way appropriate for its intention or meaning. There is no hard-and-fast rule regarding what the Levels display should look like for any image. By and large, if the image is convincing or looks excellent, its Levels will also be fine.

However, a low-resolution image may display a Levels histogram that is broken up like a comb with many gaps between the peaks. This shows there's either a poverty of image data or that the image is extremely noisy,, or both. An image that shows such a Levels histogram is not automatically to be disqualified, but its low technical quality may limit its usefulness for exhibition.

Tonality

The vast majority of images show normal tonality. This means that all tones, or brightness levels, ranging from very dark to very light can be found in the image. This does not mean that the tones are evenly distributed, but that there are few, if any, gaps in the distribution of tones. We see this in images made in normal lighting conditions such as daylight scenes. In some conditions, such as stars or street lamps at night we would expect to see uneven tone distribution. There is likely to be lots of black (Levels heaped up to the left of a histogram display) with a few points of highlight but with little else in between. That, too, is normal - for the subject.

In short, normal tonality is about reproducing the range of brightness values in the scene with a matching, and appropriate distribution in the image. Of course, what is appropriate is exactly what is open to the photographer's creative or technical interpretation. In the digital era, we have largely left behind the limitations forced on us by analogue film with their narrowly limited range of sensitivities. In addition, local tone adjustments can now be much more varied that ever before.

One result is that we now accept a wide range of tonal rendition from very flat or soft to high contrast over a wide range of genres. As a result, the range of what is acceptable in tonality runs a wide gamut.

Image sharpness

The fundamental need for good sharpness in an image does not imply that the whole of the image needs to be sharp. Rather it means that what should be sharp is in fact sharp or even very sharp.

In many images, the area that is actually sharp maybe only a single percent of the entire image, for example, the eyelashes of a close-up portrait. By 'sharp' we mean that details are resolved to good contrast with well-defined, clean boundaries.

Note that, due to limited depth of field, much of the image may be blurry and unsharp but the image as a whole will be considered to be sharp so long as the important element or key part of the subject appears sharp. There are five main causes of unsharpness or blur in images, any of which indicates lack of technical control:

- **inaccurate focus** due to movement in subject or camera after focusing, or due to inaccurate autofocusing calibration, or simply due to focusing error by the photographer

- **movement during exposure** from the subject on camera, or both

- **poor quality optics** are intrinsically unable to produce a sharp image

- **a low-resolution image** that has been enlarged beyond its pixel capacity

- **image processing** such as the application of filters or poor compositing may cause unsharpness

In the search for sharpness, it is possible to over sharpen by using image manipulation tools such as unsharp mask. This is best avoided unless it is part of the expression of the image.

Image colour

The colour standards of the past, based on the rigid reproduction qualities of colour film, do indeed lie in the past. In our era of digital photography, we work with and accept a very wide range of ways to render colour.

Today, we do not ask for colour reproduction to be accurate but merely for it to be artistically or technically appropriate to the subject or style of photography. We accept wedding photographs with cross-processed colour distortions, with pale tints and unnatural colours, but also with accurate or normal colour reproduction. Travel photographs can range from lightly tinted through to highly saturated, and with white balance ranging from accurate to deliberately set to give strong colour casts for illustrative effect.

The extent to which colours are allowed to be inaccurate or not true to life will depend on the competition rules and the norms set by the genre. In sports photography, colour reproduction tends to be conservative i.e. the preference is for accurate reproduction. The same is true of much nature photography. But in abstract or fine art photography, extremes of colour reproduction - even the inversion of colour values - are often acceptable.

Some observations:

- Images with highly de-saturated colours may originally be black-and-white images that have been tinted or else colour images that have received a lot of image manipulation.

- Inexperienced photographers may create images with highly saturated colours. These cannot be printed although the colours may be visible on screen. Over-saturation may be an indication of poor technical control. Over-saturated images may not produce high-quality prints for exhibition.

Image artefacts

Images submitted for competitions or professional use are expected not to display obvious image artefacts such as over-sharpening, pixelation, banding (posterisatiom), or severe lens faults such as veiling flare, obvious distortions, loss of contrast due to imperfect or dirty lenses.

No image is completely free of artefacts. An useful working standard is that any artefacts visible at the low resolution at which most competition images are seen are artefacts which are too large to be acceptable. For some purposes, a photographer may deliberately pixelate portions of the image e.g. to hide the identity of a face. But easily visible artefacts are usually a sign of poor technical control, or that originals are very low resolution, that a low-quality camera was used, or over-processing e.g. to make up for under-exposure ... or any combination.

Technical dimensions

The types of artefact to look for include:

- **Pixelation**: image details are rendered as square blocks of even colour which are larger than the details to be shown.This artefact is usually caused by images of small pixel dimensions being enlarged by too much.

- **JPEG artefacts**: blocks of pixels which interrupt areas of even tone that interfere with fine detail; variations within the blocks are usually smaller than differences between adjacent blocks caused by heavy compression.

- **Halos at subject boundaries**: these appear as pale fringes or boundaries around objects and can be caused by heavy unsharp masking, by strongly applied tone mapping techniques, and by highlight/ shadow controls that have been applied too strongly or with inappropriate radius settings.

- **Posterisation**: areas of tones that should transition smoothly from one colour or tone to another are rendered into bands of colour, with distinct edges between tones. This is caused by insufficient image data. It is a form of aliasing.

- **Aliasing**: curved or sloping lines are rendered with jagged or saw-toothed edges. This is also caused by lack of image data to produce clean lines. In modern high-resolution images, this defect is usually visible only when viewing the image at high magnification.

- **Optical defects and aberrations**: these range from flare and internal reflections which result from the way the lenses used, to distortions and colour fringing which are due to lens aberrations or defects in lens design. Modern lenses are highly corrected for aberration, so optical defects may be due to mistakes by the camera operator or may be deliberately applied by the photographer.

Image noise

In the early days of digital photography, the problem of noisy images of lowlight scenes was a major preoccupation for the good reason that it was a major cause of poor image quality. This showed up not only as irregular patterns of pixels that disrupted subject detail, colours were poor and dynamic range (ability to render a range of tones from brightest to darkest) was limited.

With today's sensor technology, larger sensors and much improved image processing, image noise is much less of a problem. Whereas ISO settings of greater than 400 were avoided because they caused visibly noisy images, ISO settings of 16000 (sixteen thousand) or greater can now be used without much reservation. This means that the photographers are able to work in ever lower light conditions.

Modern images that exhibit visible noise - pixels in the image which are unrelated to the details on the subject - are often images that have received heavy image manipulation in a form of shadow recovery or tone-mapping operations.

- **Easily visible noise** may be a sign of heavy cropping or over-enlargement or high levels of image compression used to reduce file size.

- **Post-processing** may cause noise, through attempts to recover shadow detail or correct under-exposure, possibly also from over-sharpening.

- **Images processed to simulate film grain** may appear to be noisy when they have been reduced in size for viewing or submission to a competition. The reduction in resolution mixes up the 'grain' structure to make it look like noise.

Subject alignment

The norm is for images to be lined up in the frame so that the horizon is level or horizontal, and for vertical lines to be lined up vertically and in parallel.

How precisely an image should line up with horizon or vertical depends in part on individual taste and in part on the photojudging. In architecture, it's obvious that the norm is for precision in the rendering of horizons and verticals: small deviations are signs of poor technical control. With landscape photography however, there is some latitude for sloping horizons or verticals: what is permissible is very much a matter of taste. With feature, travel, editorial fashion photography, strongly sloping horizontals or verticals may be entirely acceptable.

In general, small or just-noticeable sloping horizons or verticals indicate imprecise technical or editing control.

A related issue is the convergence of parallels when photographing from an angle. This most often seen in photographs of buildings where the camera looks upwards to take in the full height. As with horizons, very small convergences may be tolerated, while more easily visible convergences may reveal poor technique or lack of quality control. This is likely true as modern image manipulation software enables even strong convergence to be corrected convincingly.

On the other hand, very strong or obvious convergence, often used together with slanted horizons, is usually accepted being intentional.

Bear in mind that contemporary design fashion favours letter-box or panorama-shaped images i.e. wide and narrow top to bottom e.g. 16:9 or 4:1. These proportions tend to exaggerate any error in the horizon, so what may have been slight tilt with squarer formats such as 3:4 or 2:3 may appear more obvious in letter-box formats.

A strong tilt of the horizon (*top, right*) appears appropriate to the action on the container wharf. But the slight tilt of the horizon in an image with many straight lines (*middle, right*) is not so convincing. The tilt in the horizon may not be a problem, the cranes being off-vertical may be more disturbing.

A slight up-ward view of the monument in Uzbekistan (*below, left*) causes the tower to tilt but is acceptable.
The strong upward and slanted view of open windows (*below, right*) is also acceptable as a visual gesture.

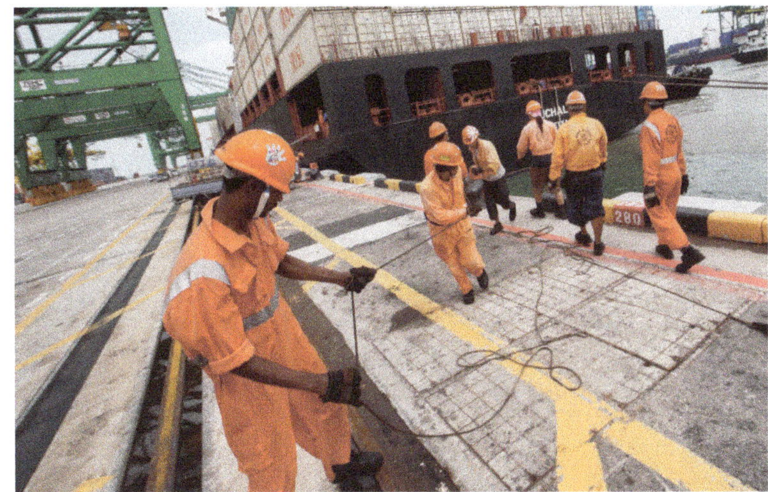

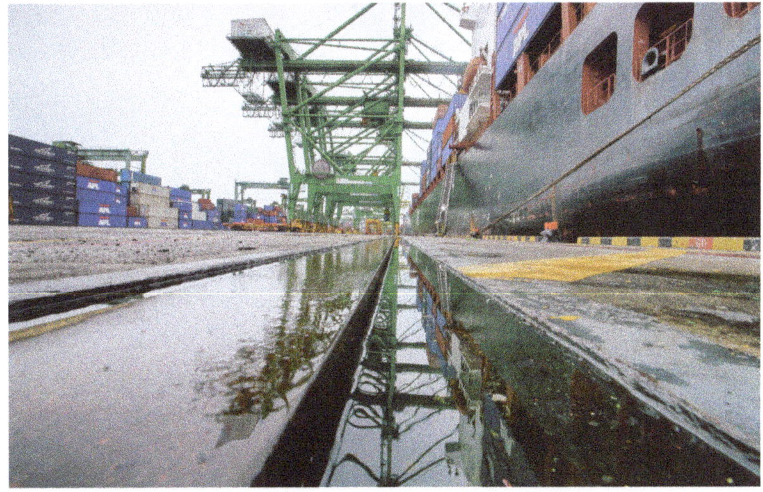

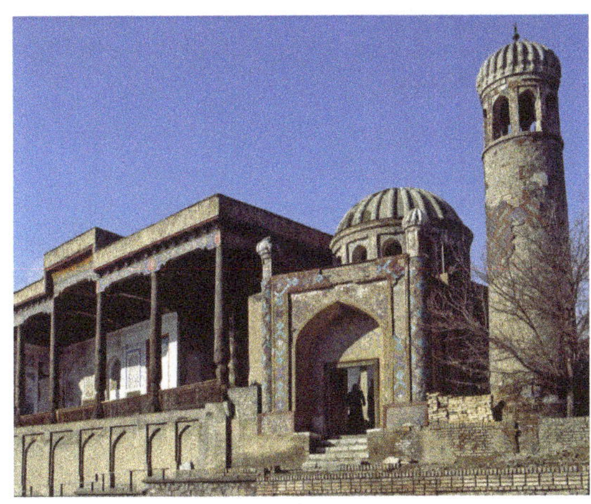

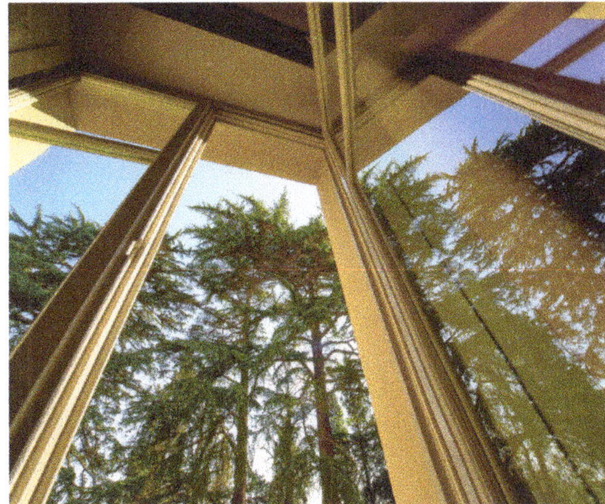

Aesthetic dimension

AS A JUDGE OF PHOTOGRAPHY, whether it's your own or those of others, the greater your visual experience and knowledge, the greater the insightfulness and subtlety you can apply to forming an opinion about an image.

No amount of writing or debate about the image can substitute for deep experience of a wide spectrum of images. This means that you best prepare yourself by spending days and days looking at great photography: all of it, from the past through to the present. It also means consuming from a wide range of sources: from fashion magazines to news papers, through to classic monographs, and histories of photography. It means sourcing from fine art galleries and museums to social media postings, looking at different uses of images from the scientific record to fantasy composites. Furthermore, ensure you sample from all over the world - Middle East, Far East, Africa as well as Europe and North America.

We could say you'll be making progress when you've looked carefully at 10,000 images.

With greater experience, your understanding of how you respond to images will inform that experience and deepen your engagement. The more your learn of images from every possible source, the more you develop a faculty to view critically. You will also be informed by awareness of photographic and art history, and of cultural, even political history. As you expose yourself to a wider range of imagery, your ability to understand the intentions of a wide range of photography will increase. This is the foundation for fair, knowledgeable and open judgement of images.

Without such a foundation, your selection of images will serve only to reinforce a limited worldview of images. When unused to challenge, you have the potential to wind in ever-tighter circles around the same, limited and undiversified centre of

visual culture. In this chapter, we can't replace an
life-time's visual education, but here are some
suggestions to help you get started:

- **Consume, digest, analyse images** instead of merely
  looking at them: treat all images as opportunities to
  learn about how an image works, why it was used,
  what cultural and aesthetic dynamic is at work.

- **Consume all visual culture,** not only photographs: but
  also painting, sculpture, architecture from all over the
  world. Advertising, street art, fashion, kitsch: all serve
  to inform your eye.

- **Look at magazines, illustrated books, web pages** to
  see how and why images are used: ask yourself why
  some are more effective than others.

Representation

To a surprising degree, the precise subject or scene
represented in an image is usually only of secondary
importance either to its usefulness or its award-
winning qualities. In wedding photography, for
instance, the happy couple are essentially
anonymous - metaphorically faceless - for the
purposes of judging an image for a competition. The
factors that count are the staging, the lighting, the
use of props and imaginative posing of the subjects,
and so on. These qualities function independently
of the two people being photographed. Whether
they are young or old, Asian or African or
Polynesian, is largely immaterial. Mostly, what
matters is the skill exercised in photographing the
wedding couple.

Photojournalism or news offers a sharp contrast.
If the subject or scene is sufficiently important,
dramatic or the moment is truly revelatory, it may
not matter at all if the technical quality is low or

that aesthetic flair is missing. The image would still be regarded as outstanding.

In general, the greater control we have when photographing, the higher our expectations for the creativity, innovativeness, and control of the technical dimension. This applies equally to a wide range of photographic subjects, from landscapes to studio portraiture, from still life to the architecture. Inversely, where the photographic situation cannot be controlled, as in conflict zones, family documentary or news, we tend to lower our expectations of technical qualities in favour of the genuine capture of an important event.

An image may also be chosen because it fulfils some peripheral function. For instance, suppose the choice of winner of a competition is between an attractive portrait of a charming child and an abstract still life hinting at war and devastation from an abandoned building. Now, suppose the winning picture is to be used on large posters to promote the competition sponsors,. It's pretty obvious which image would be preferred by the press relations and marketing people. Whether this influences decisions made by the photojudges is a matter for the management of a competition.

Composition

This aspect of the image is often one given close, if not obsessive, attention by many photographers. Yet, an image's composition is seldom sufficient in itself to guarantee that it is remarkable or prize-winning in any way. Nonetheless, a strong, interesting or innovative composition is an important factor for some genres of photography such as travel, landscape and nature. In some types of photography, clever composition may almost be frowned upon as step too far towards commodification - making it look attractive to make more desirable - as in news photography. In these genres, the stylistic preference is for straightforward, or objective - even bland - presentations of the subject.

In subject areas where composition makes an important contribution to the quality and appeal of an image, there are some of the factors you can use in arriving at a judgement or assessment:

- **Accuracy of placement:** elements in well-composed images look as if they have been carefully positioned: the horizon in just the right place, the main subject at just the right proportion of the frame, the overall shapes of space between subjects appearing carefully designed.

- **Care taken in composition:** images tend show 'correct' space between elements within the image and between elements and the edge of the frame. Objects, such as lamp-posts or faces which are placed so close to the picture frame that they appear to 'kiss' or objects in the background that appear to nearly touch a face: these may count as signs indicating a poor control of the image's composition.

- **Simple composition:** Images which have been very simply composed, for example with the main subject placed centrally or the horizon through the centre of the image, are not necessarily poorly composed or poor images. While they may 'break' certain rules for some photographers, they may actually be composed to show the subject in the most economical, effective way.

- **Full use of frame:** strongly composed images tend to make full use of the frame, with dynamic elements and active space extending into all corners, filling the picture space. This does not mean the image is full of details but that the picture frame is exploited to the edges and corners, often with the suggestion there's more going on beyond the confines of the frame.

Narrative

The narrativic element in a single image is the story that is implied or hinted at by elements in the photograph. As a single image is a still photograph that records only a thin slice of time, any storytelling that takes place over time can only be suggested by what is shown in the image, working together with the viewer to fill in the gaps.

As a result, the power of the narrative content of an image depends heavily on additional information external to the image. This may be provided directly through caption information, and through knowledge brought to the image by the viewer e.g. when the viewer recognises faces shown in an image. Or viewers obtain extra information through its relationship of the image to other images, which may neighbouring images in a sequence or panel. (See also Panel sequencing from p.98.)

In judging the narrative content of an image, judges should be expert in the subject. For example, suppose we have an image of a couple holding hands against a sunset on a tropical beach. In one context, it could be a commercial holiday image suitable for stock photography. But in the context of wedding photography, it shows a couple on their honeymoon. For an article on global warming - the very same image could suggest that by the time the couple's children are grown up, the scene will be impossible as it will be under water.

Points for picture judges to consider regarding the narrative content of images include:

- If there is any uncertainty over interpreting the narrative, ask for additional information.

- If the image is of a subject that you are not expert on, ask for expert guidance. Specialist subjects such as wildlife, sports etc. are best left to those with the knowledge to read the images correctly.

- If the image is part of a sequence or panel, its narrative content s important to appreciate in order to understand the sequence as a whole.

Communication

Any image that survives the very fine filtration process of editing is an image that has succeeded in communicating an idea or feeling. Such an image will have used all the features we have discussed .

It can be shown to have blended factors from the whole toolkit of ways to express, together with technical control, to achieve at least the following:

- **Present the subject or idea with clarity:** the subject is easy to identify: it is clear, simple, perhaps colourful and direct, even if the main subject is abstract or an emotion.

- **Communicate sense of connection with subject:** associativity is the property of the image which enables the viewer to relate to, or sympathise with, or empathise with the feelings expressed in the image through viewing it.

- **Create sense of movement and narrative within frame:** the composition of elements in the image has a primary role in encouraging the viewer to explore the image and to uncover its narrative content. This contributes to the interestingness of the image.

- **Motivate examination:** interestingness is the quality of the image which encourages viewers to look closely or explore or think about what the image is expressing. Without interestingness, or some feature of the image that attracts attention, the image is not likely to have much of a future in front of the public.

Excitement

All the technical control and aesthetic mastery would count for almost nothing if the resulting image did not create some sense of excitement. For an image to succeed in competitions, it must stand out from the immediate crowd of thousands of other images. When judging large competitions, judges may spend less than three seconds looking at each image in the pressing knowledge that they may have several hundred images to evaluate by the end of the day. If an image does not catch their attention at once, it is passed over. Winning images are those that not only catch but also hold the attention, and invite deeper exploration.

Technically perfect images of wonderful subjects need some extra dimensions in today's world in which nearly 3,000,000,000,000 (yes; that's three trillion) images are produced each year if they have any hope of standing out and catching judges' attention. These may include:

- **Astonish, startle or surprise:** the viewer should respond viscerally, with excitement because something in the image comes across as original, striking or thrilling. I call it 'falling in love': why award a prize to an image that hasn't grabbed your heart?

- **Engage viewers:** through its newness, revelatory qualities or addition to experience or knowledge.

- **Insight into the subject** in ways that draws the viewer into the image to explore and discover more.

- **Convince viewers:** through following a line of engaged, committed, logical enquiry that is visually coherent, profoundly seen and sympathetic to the subject - particularly important for sequences or picture essays.

- **Resonate with viewer emotions:** images that communicate the photographer's love and empathetic commitment to his or her subject in ways which the viewer can understand or identify with and thus share the subject's or the photographer's feelings.

- **Images may intrigue viewers:** without being too obvious or explicit because subtle visual illusions or symbolism create a depth of meanings or suggestions which invite viewers to ponder or think on a proposition (that may come from a title or caption), or to share some emotion.

- **Image power:** derives from offering a multi-level richness of visual, conceptual, intellectual experience that extend beyond the obvious, superficial or immediate visual impact.

- **Historical moment:** an image that captures a key moment in history such as a kiss at a Royal Wedding, the storming of the Capitol building, may be exciting simply because it reminds the viewer of a key event in their lifetime.

THE SMALL NUMBER OF VISUAL EXAMPLES in this book is deliberate. I have no intention of showing or telling you what should or should not be in a photograph. Nor to instruct you as to which way to communicate is correct, or better or not.

My view is that competitions and awards are with us to encourage invention, innovation and courageous vision, not to reward the safe reworking of tired themes and approaches. This is not achieved by constraining or promoting my, or anyone else's, ideas of what is effective in photography. There is already a strong tendency for competitions to reinforce and perpetuate norms and visual habits.

These exercises aim to start you thinking about your own visual as well as your visceral reactions. To start you analysing your responses to images and relate your responses to those of others. Interrogate yourself at all times. If someone were to ask you 'Why did you make that face? Why did you shake your head?' be ready to give a honest reply.

Look at the images and ask yourself:

- **What is it - exactly** - about an image that makes you like it (or not)?

- **Which kinds of treatment or subject** would you dislike however well the image was constructed?

- **Which features do you have a natural preference for** - textures, monochrome, nudes, etc. - that you may need to be aware of?

- **Even if you detest** the subject matter or approach would you be able to recognise high quality when judged by more objective standards?

- **Actively evaluate your responses:** as your experience grows, so will your ability to articulate your responses and the reasons for them.

ATTRACTION

Which of these portraits do you find most interesting? Or the most attractive? Do you like the person depicted. Which image was the first to catch your eye? Explain why.

- Are you influenced by the subject itself?

- Are you influenced by eye contact or by its lack?

- Do you find softness of texture preferable to harder textures?

- Do you find strong colours distracting, compared to monochrome colours?

- Which image (if any) would be much improved by conversion to black-and-white?

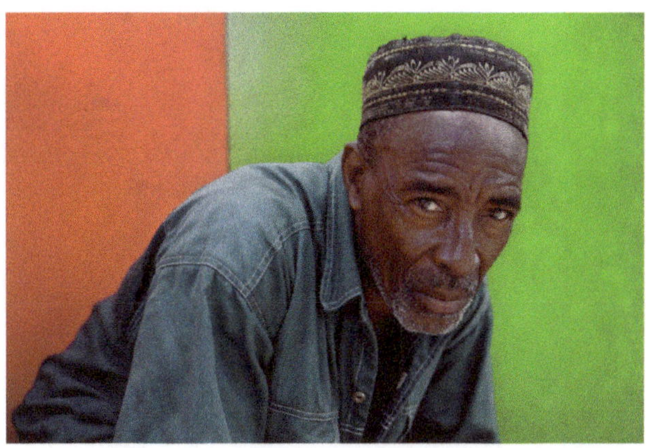

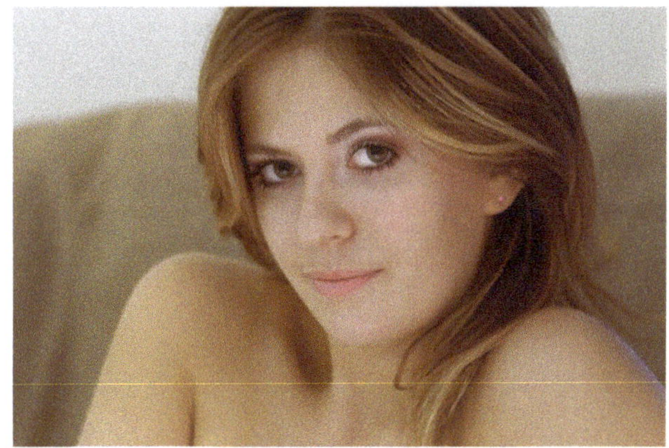

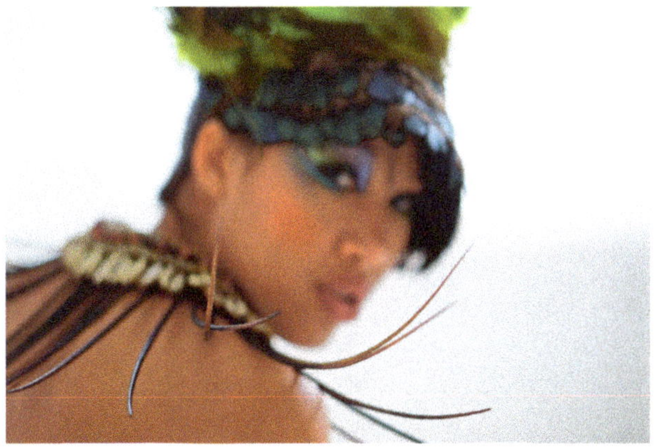

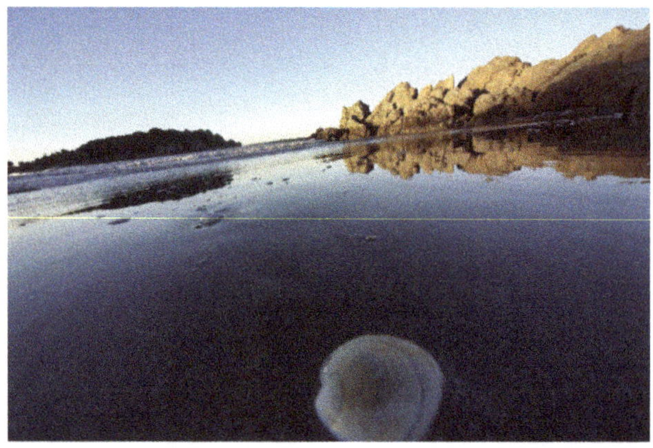

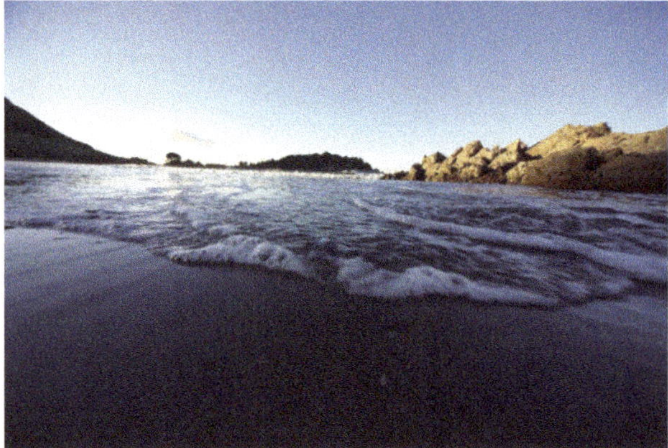

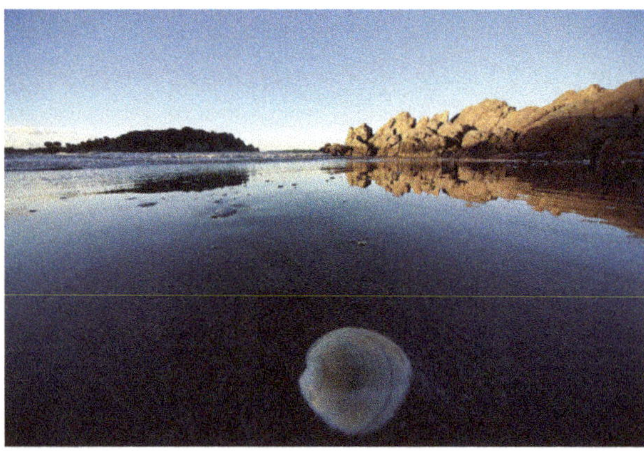

HORIZONS

Assess the choice of orientation of horizon in these images.

- Does it make any difference to the impact of the image how much the horizon slopes? If so, why? And if not, why not? Does the answer depend on the subject matter?

- Does a small error in horizontal appear to you to be an accident or a sign of poor technical control?

- Does a strong angled slant look contrived?

- Does a level horizon look rather boring and predictable?

- Of these images, which one works best? Explain why.

See also pp.76-7.

TAKE YOUR PICK

Which of these variants do you find most the successful or convincing? Which would be your choice for publication?

- Examine the position of the model.

- Examine the position of the lamp and how it illuminates her face.

- Assess the overall exposure and colour balance.

- Examine the lighting from the right and how well it balances with the rest of the hallway.

- Examine the trail of light: which is most interesting? Also check out the lighting on the stairs.

- Examine the lighting in the background: is it better if it's all dark or with some light?

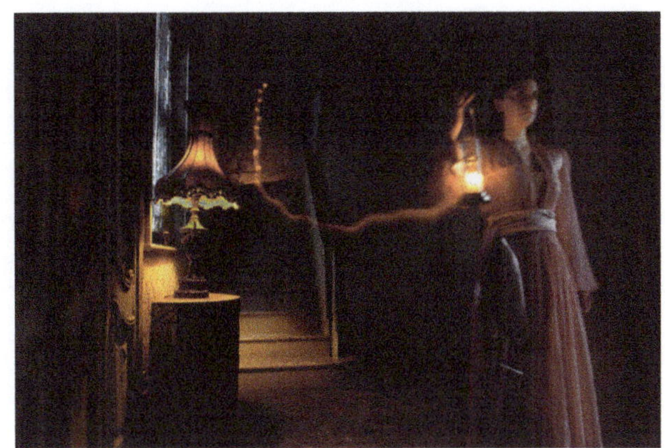

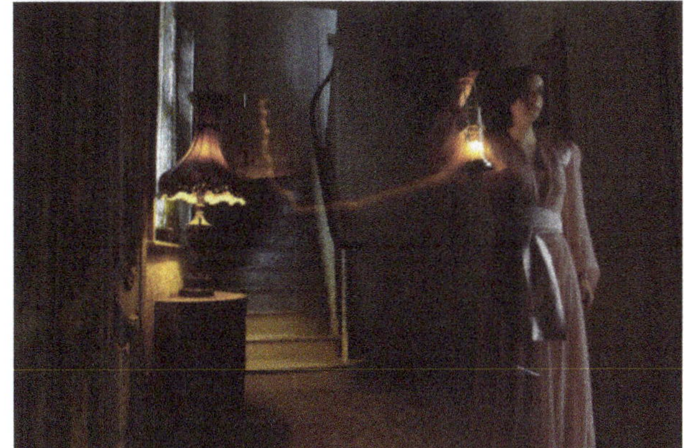

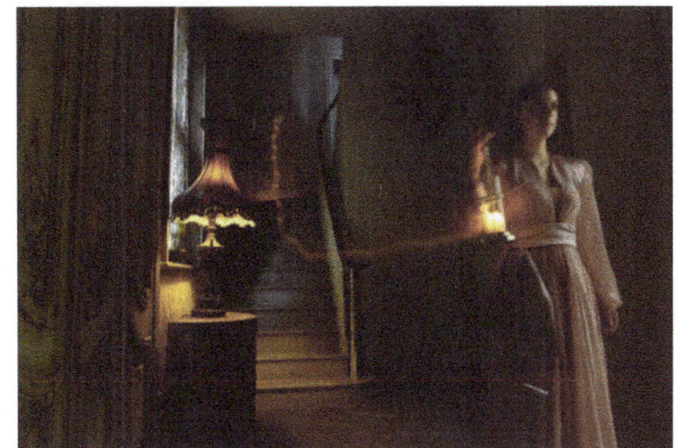

ELIMINATE

Identify the two images out of these nine that do not belong to the set. Then make a balanced sequence of the remaining images for a travel feature about the destination. This exercise is aimed at leading you to question the subject-matter independently of the quality of the photography.

- Is there something missing? What kind of image would you look for to improve the variety in the sequence?

- If you think there's an obviously weak image, why do you think so? And with what kind of image would you replace it?

- *Clue*: one image has been processed markedly differently from the others and comes from a different country from the majority. The other doesn't fit either geographically, nor architecturally.

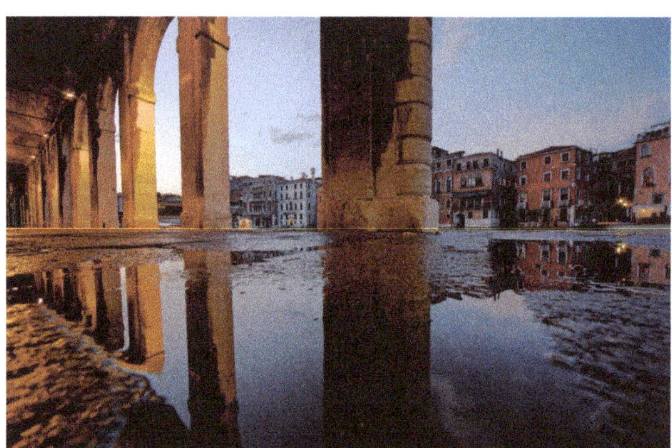

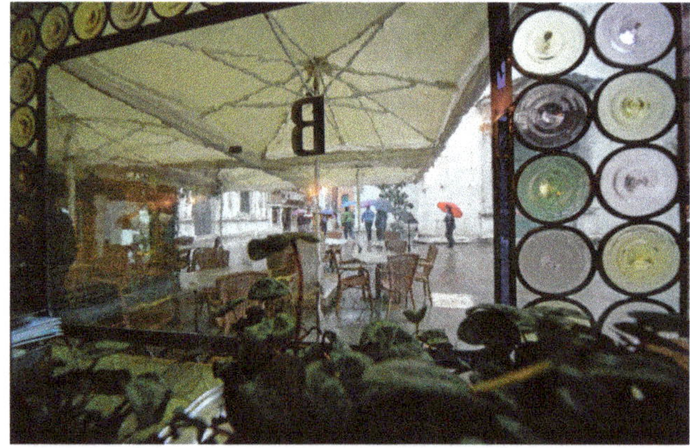

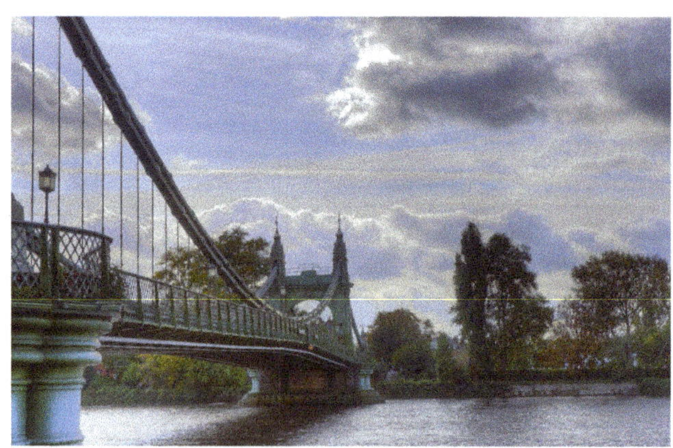

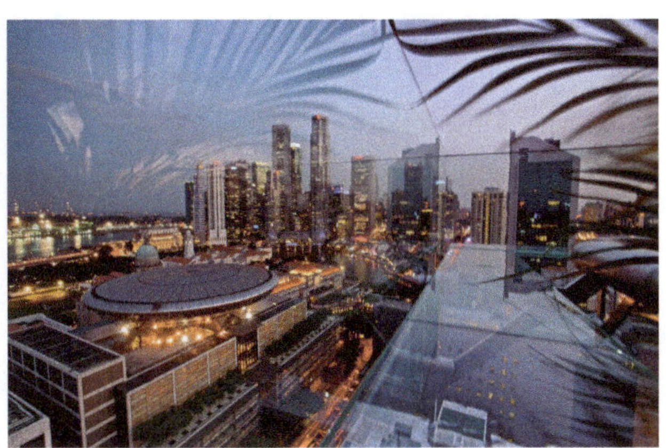

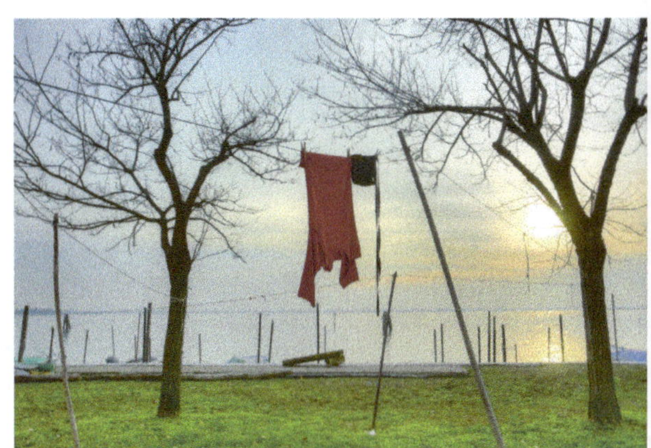

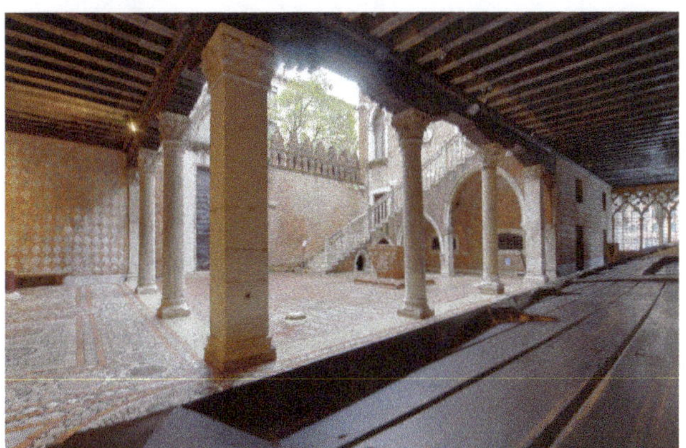

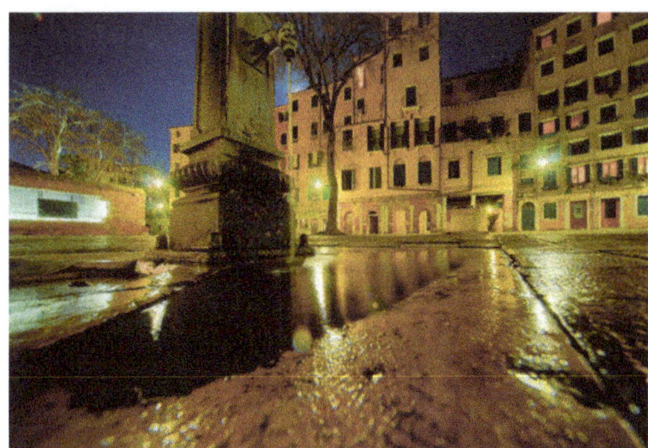

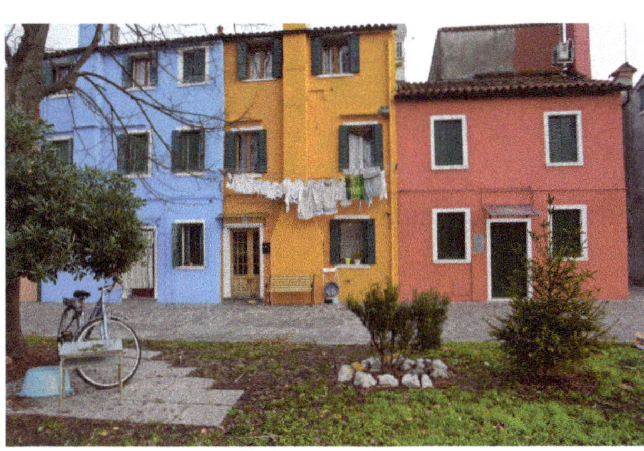

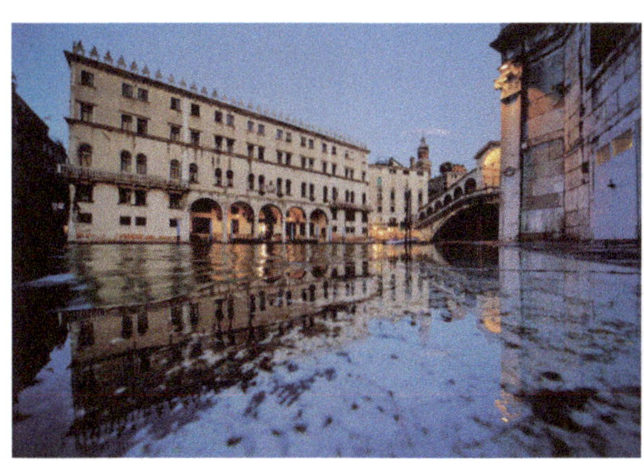

UNRETOUCHED?

In each of these images, the photographers claim to have applied only tonal and colour or to have made a black-and-white conversion. Is that true? If not, which image manipulation effects have been used, and what's your evidence?

Clues to observe include:

- lighting that doesn't look natural

- shadows that fall oddly

- vertical lines where you'd expect to see slanted lines

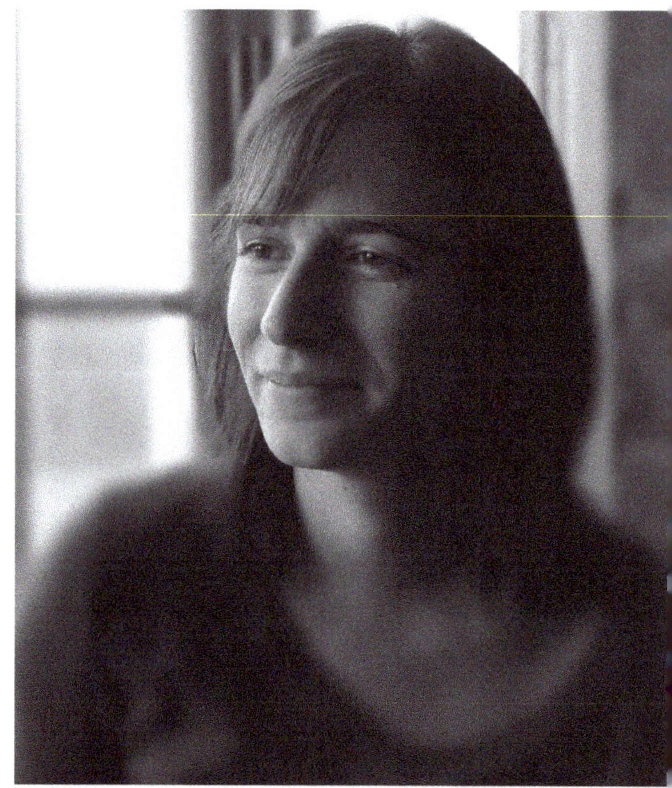

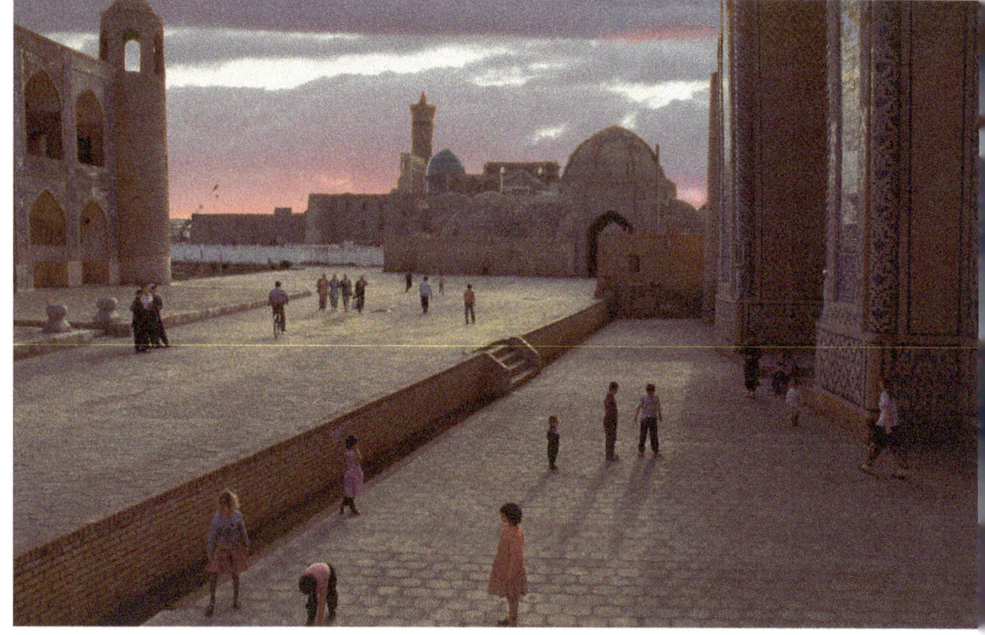

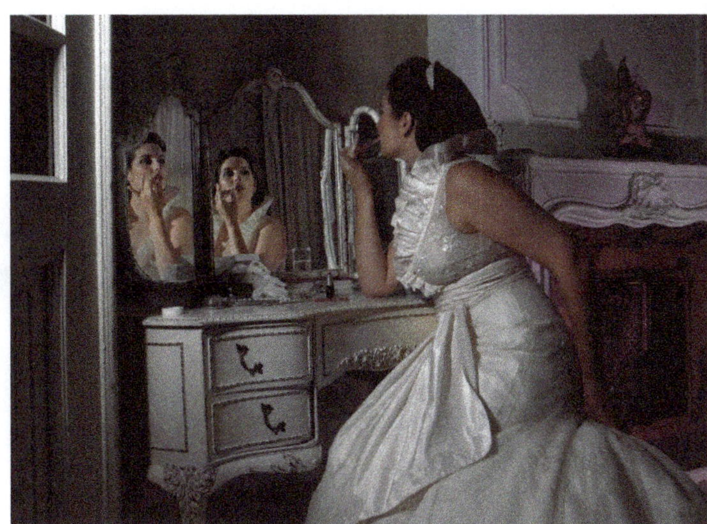

- colours that appear too saturated or incorrect colour balance compared to the rest of the image

Take a good look at these images and decide which were made in-camera and which were post-processed.

Answers

- **Top left (opposite):** retouched with Gaussian blur on selections.

- **Bottom left (opposite):** composite with sky from another location.

- **Top (right):** in-camera with only tweak of levels and colour balance.

- **Middle (right):** retouched with distortion tools to correct verticals slanted by looking up and to the right of the building.

- **Bottom (right):** in camera, no retouching. Image shows reflection of clouds on shop window with interior lighting.

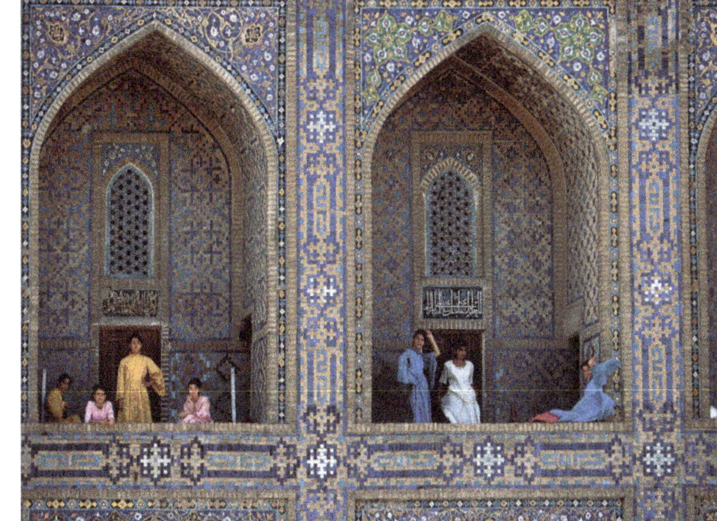

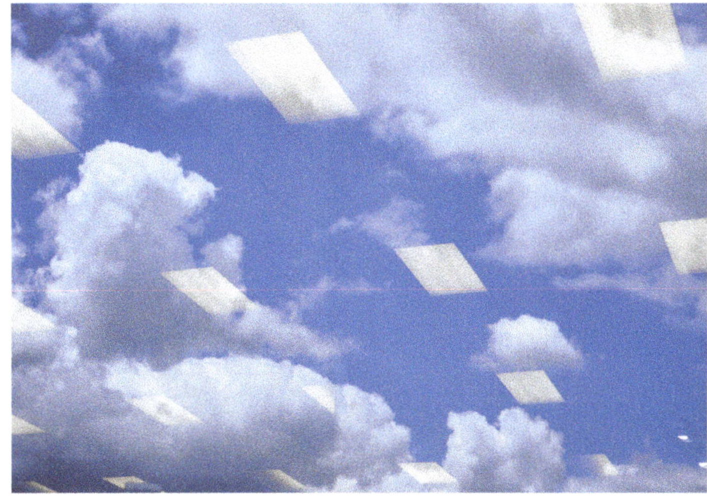

COMPOSITION

Which compositional techniques are used in these images and how do they work? Which do you find attract your attention? Which do you find dull and predicatable? Are any of the techniques used here ones that you would never use? If so, why?

- Do you look for simplicity or do you prefer complicated arrangements?

- Do you prefer a single, clearly defined subject, or an amalgamation of different elements?

- Do you try to visualise how each image at different sizes? Which images would be more effective if they were much larger? Which ones may appear to be weak when seen at large sizes?

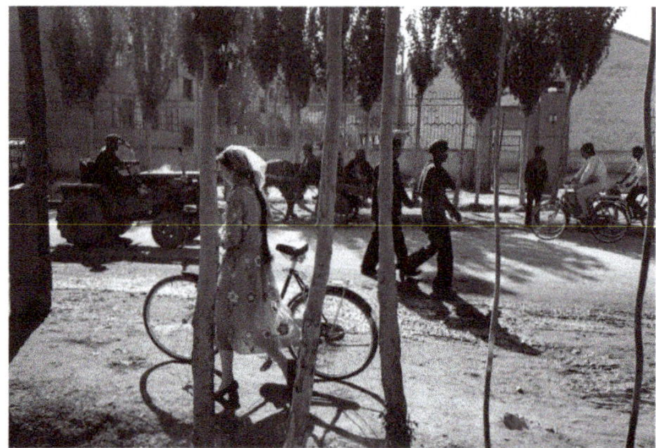

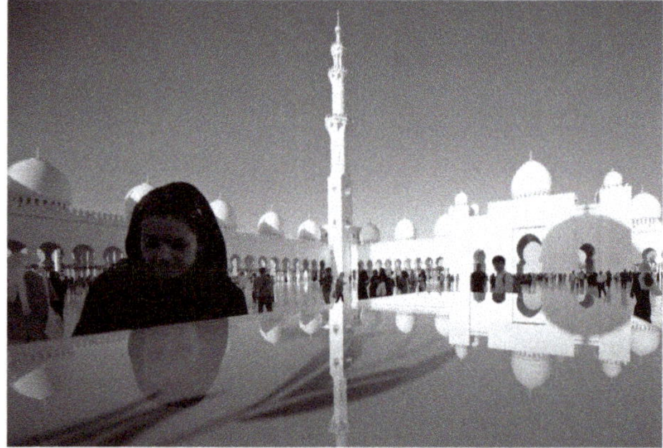

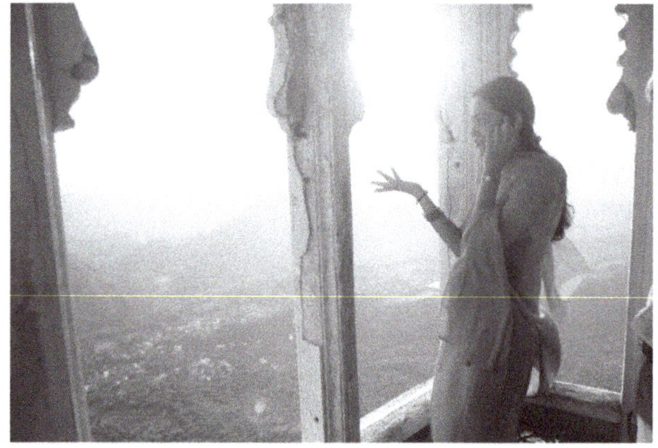

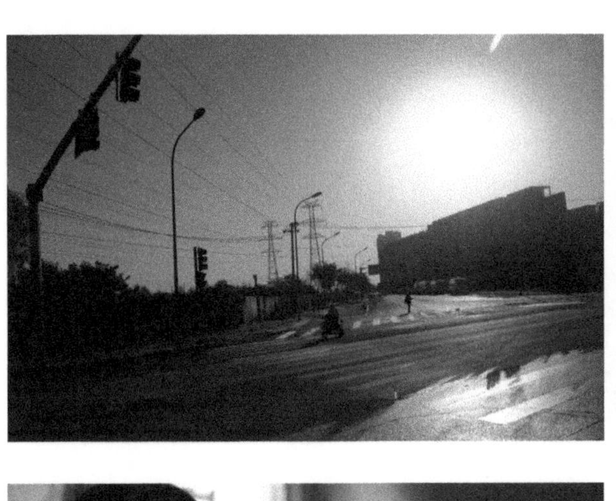
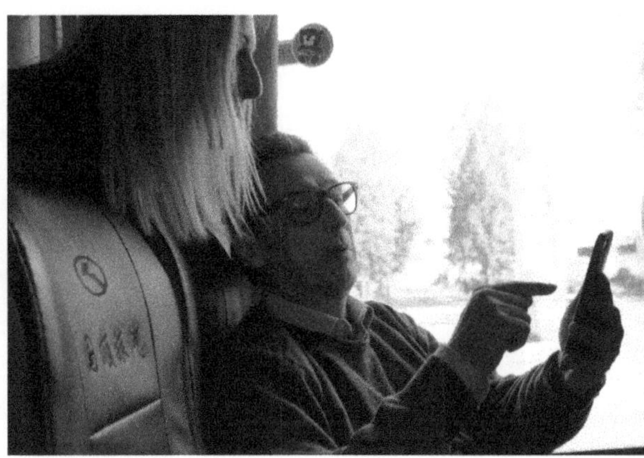
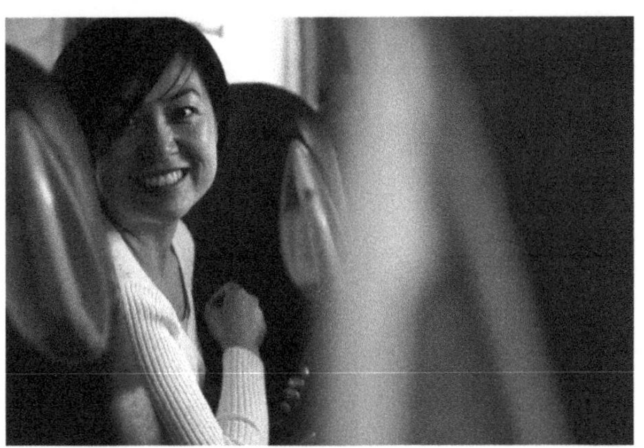
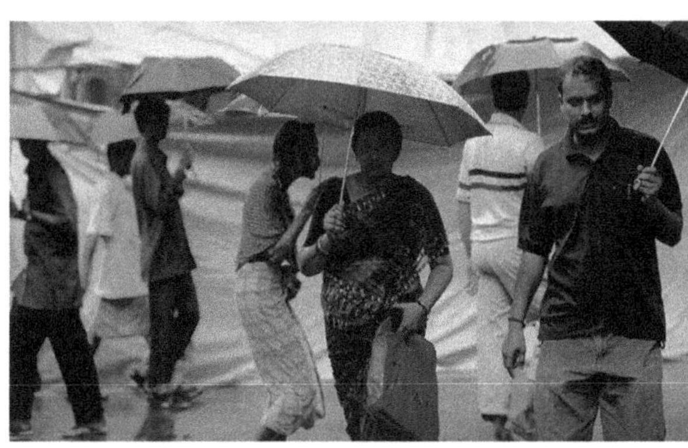
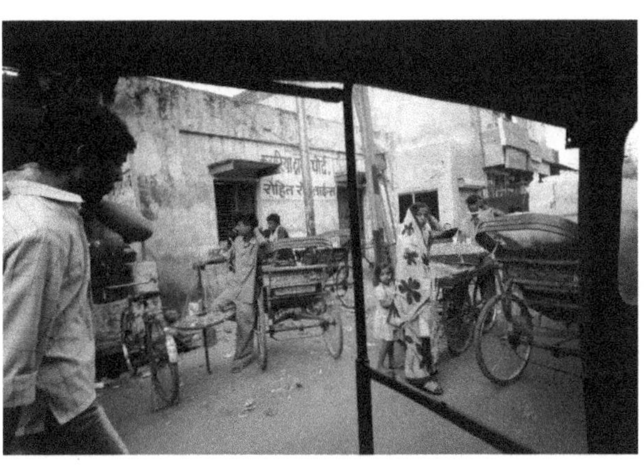
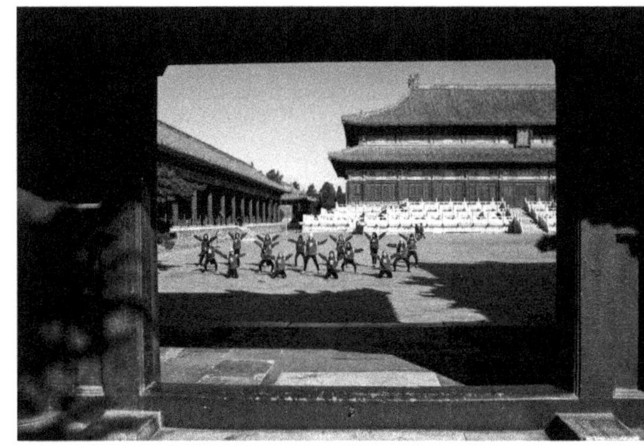

USE OF COLOUR

Some of these images use different hues economically, others help themselves generously to the entire colour palette. Which work best, which catch the attention? Is it only to do with colour?

- Do subtle contrasts work better than a strong and rich variety?

- What happens when one colour overpowers the others ... and which colour seems the strongest?

- Examine the role of neutral colours i.e. greys and blacks in providing context and ground for bright colours.

- How important that skin tone and skin colour are accurate?

- Are colours more effective if they are more saturated? What if they are less saturated than they should be? Or if they are more saturated than normal?

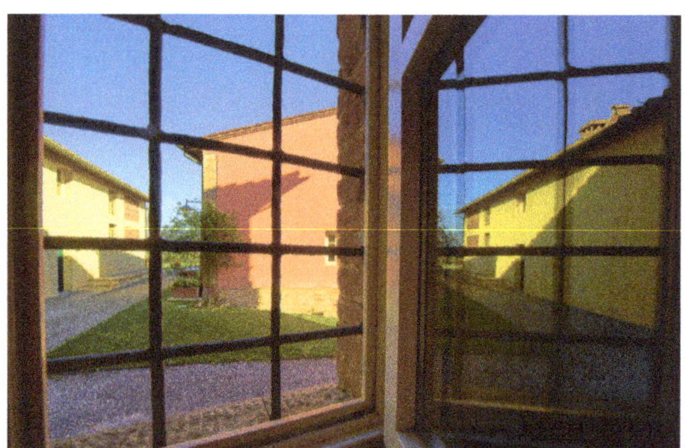

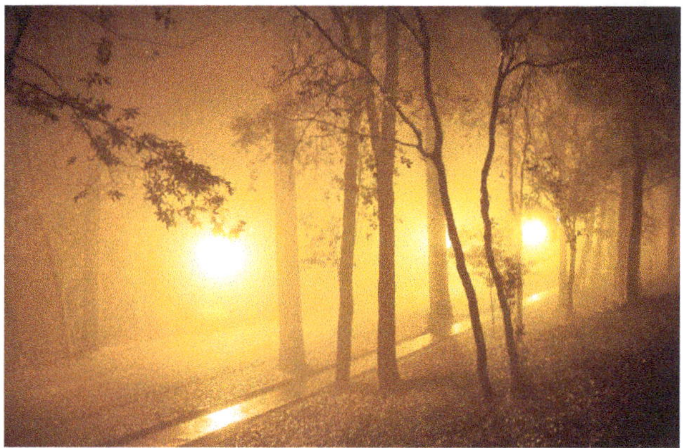

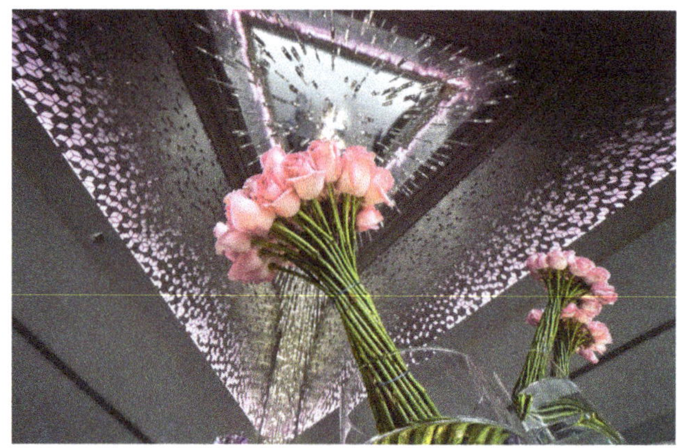

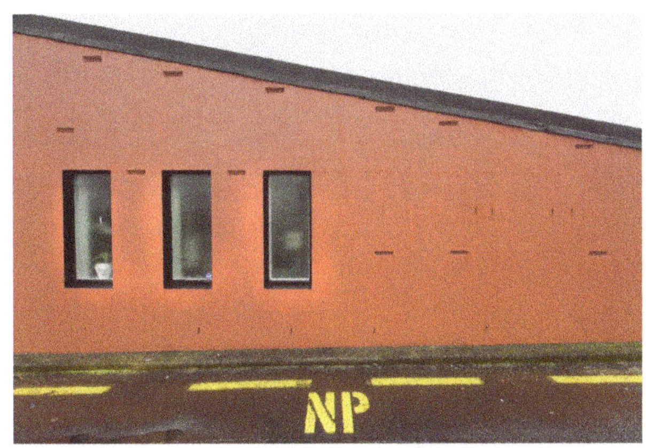
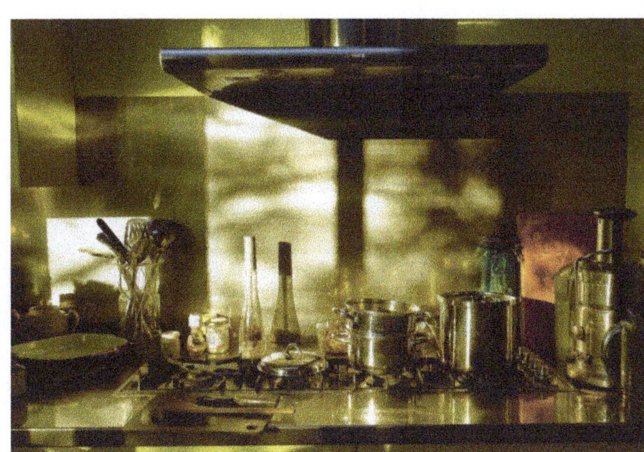
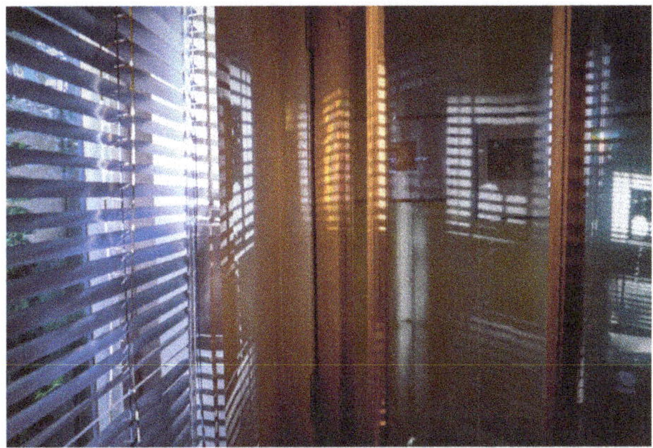
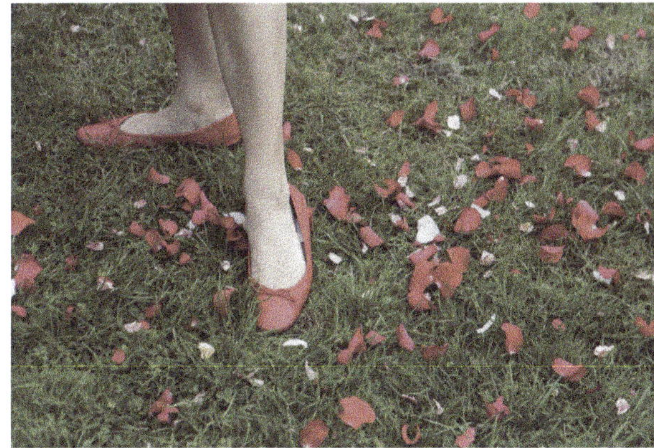
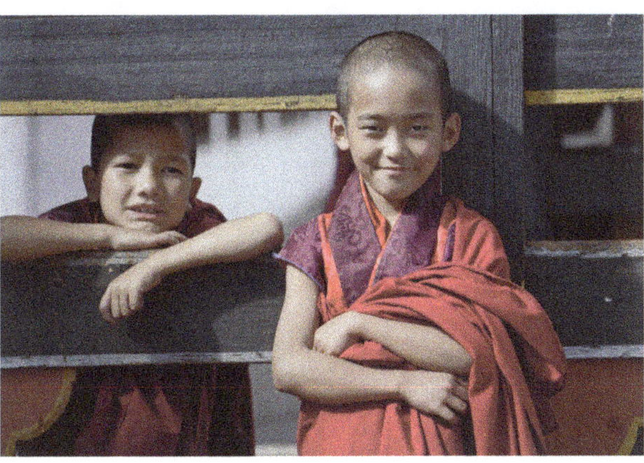
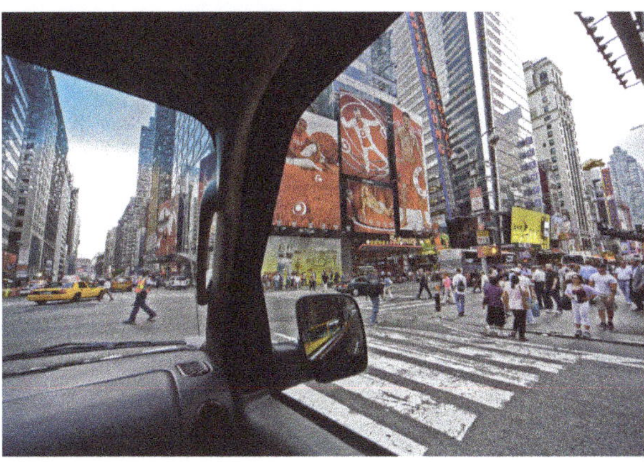

Panel sequencing

IN REAL LIFE, images are seldom seen in isolation. Much of the time, images are randomly mixed. But when a group of related images are seen together they may take on an extra dimension of meaning. The images give each other visual support, fill in the context. In short, the totality can be much greater than the individual parts taken separately.

The advantages of combining a number of related images has been well developed in the art of magazine picture essays. Well-curated exhibitions are very much about careful combinations and sequencing between images.

Many photographic competitions and awards recognise the importance of groups of pictures or panels, and may run special sections that reward panels of pictures. These groups or panels of images may be loosely associated i.e. the order of hanging is not critical. Alternatively the order may be crucial; these are sequences of images, not merely a grouping.

The presentation of a number of works in a group, panel or sequence calls for a higher level of appreciation than normal. Judges are expected to assess the group as a whole, judge inter-relationships between images as well as individual images. This assessment involves appreciating the structure of the group or sequence as a whole and how that relates to the narrative referred to.

Narrative

The narrative qualities of a panel of images, also known as its narrativity, consists of the processes used by the photographer to present a connected sequence of images, It shapes how a viewer perceives the narrative. Taken in isolation, a single image of, say, a seabird doesn't lead naturally towards a specific narrative. If you have a sequence of five different seabirds, you can conclude that you have a sequence designed to show different species. But if you're presented with pictures of the same seabird species, but taken at different stages of its life, then it's clear that narrative is bird's life story.

Another notion that fits here is that of the theme. This may be a concept that runs through the images and unifies all. The notion of theme allows for a much broader mix of images than that of a narrative. For example, take the theme of flight. Images could show scenes in airports, people running away, seabirds flying, fantasies from flights of imagination. All could be argued to arise from the same theme.

How a judge assesses these sets of images will depend on the narrative or theme they claim to represent. For example, if we are being shown five different birds, we would expect to see images that show species characteristics clearly or that each image presents a very different visual statement. We would not be greatly impressed, for example, if every picture was a portrait of a bird on its nest. On the other hand, if the narrative is a life history, we do expect to see the same species in each image, but these would be rendered to give insights, show rarely observed behaviour, or dramatic moments.

Whatever the content of the narrative, judges will also look for a compelling sequencing. This means that the motion from one image to the other is visually convincing and carries the viewer from beginning to end, just like a good story.

Reading direction

Thanks to the cultural domination from the northern hemisphere, there is a general tendency to assume that picture sequences should be read from left to right. It is perfectly natural for anyone who reads texts from left to right to expect to read picture sequences in the same direction. But, of course, at least half the world's population reads from right to left, and some scan each line from top to bottom, not from side to side.

This means that image sequences that work well when read in either direction are most likely to succeed on an international stage. Besides, in a typical exhibition situation, it is hard to control the movement of visitors, so anyone could end up reading a sequence of pictures from right to left.

Consistency

In assessing a sequence of related images, every element of similarity between the images provides the foundation for variation in content. This means that judges will quickly notice if there are variations between images that interrupt the flow. They will look for technical and stylistic inconsistencies causing that obstruction. For example, the overall brightness and gamma of the images should be consistent if that is what will support the images. Or, if they do vary between images, such variations work only when convincingly appropriate to the subject of the image.

For example, in a sequence of theatre portraits, styling and stylistic consistency in terms of lighting, scale or size, type of pose, and use of backgrounds would be expected.

Or, in a sequence of landscapes, a single black-and-white image would stand out - and probably not in a commendable way - in a sequence of strongly saturated colour images.

In the case of panels of prints, consistency in presentation, such as print surface, size, and framing should be regarded as a basic. This does not necessarily mean that all images should be either landscape format or portrait. In many cases, a variety of landscape and portrait formats is acceptable, provided the overall structure and architectural integrity of the sequence is preserved. This means that the prints relate to each other in a logical and visually coherent way: the flow and movement of shapes should appear to make sense, in order to ensure the whole is greater than the sum of the components.

Variety

The extent to which images in a set or panel are different from each other is a dimension of photography that tests the photographer's artistic and editing (selection) skills. A panel of images may show a great variety of treatment at the risk of looking like a jumble of visual statements with a weak sense of story, or only loosely related to a theme. On the other hand, images which are too similar to each other may look dull, lacking in imagination and with no sense of progression. (Note that such a set, when seen from a distance, may hold together very well.)

Judges will look for a balance between variation and similarity that best suits the subject or theme. For example, if a panel represents a day in the life of a subject, the narrative that is supported by strongly visual variety is likely to do well. For example we have a wide general view followed by an extreme close-up, then a portrait, a still life, a beautifully-lit portrait indoors - there can be great visual variety but the narrative is held together by a clear theme.

Or consider a set of portraits of people brought together by an event - for example, a pro-democracy protest The series may show them all against the same black cloth background. The only difference from picture to picture is provided by the subjects themselves, so the strength of the panel rests entirely on the characters depicted. By reducing variety in visual treatment to the minimum, the photographer is making it clear that prime position goes to the subjects. In this case, uniformity of treatment is a virtue, and would not be a good reason to mark down the sequence.

SEQUENCING

The first step is to take out the image(s) you consider to be the weakest, and re-arrange the whole set to make the most effective sequence of the images. (Originals made on film in former Soviet Central Asia.)

- Take a screen-shot of each of the images and save them to your computer or tablet. Then you can show them them in different orders.

- Consider the subject-matter, direction of movement, engagement with the subject, overall shape.

- Consider the different scales of the images - from distant landscape to the subject within touching distance.

- As another exercise, try this: suppose you have to pick three images only for a short blog on Central Asia. Which three would you pick, and why?

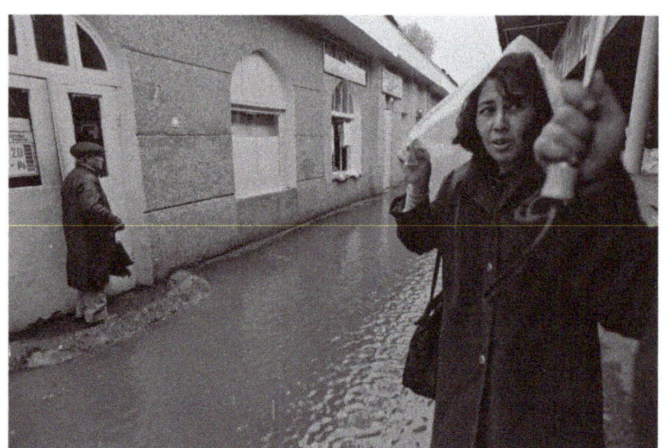

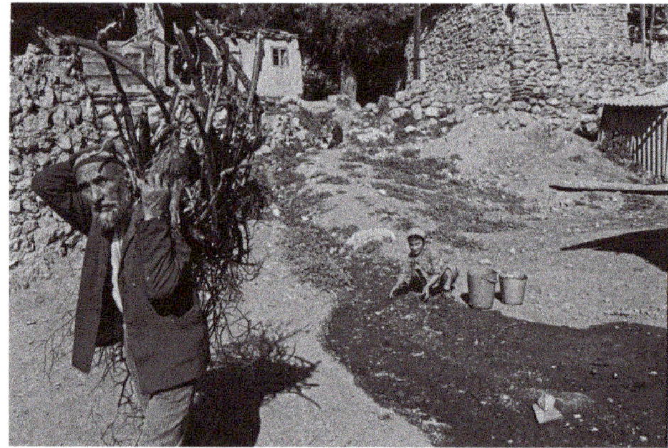

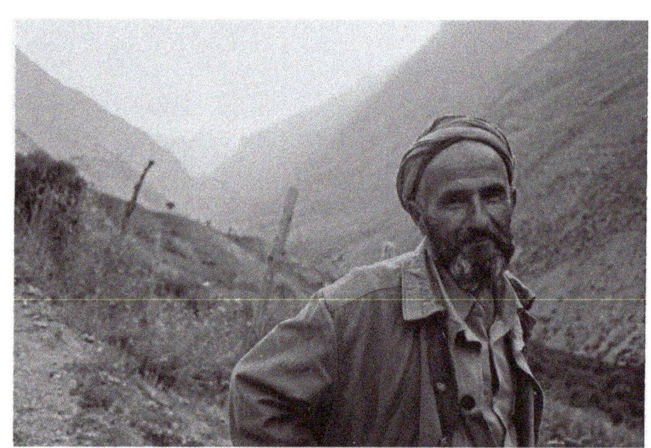

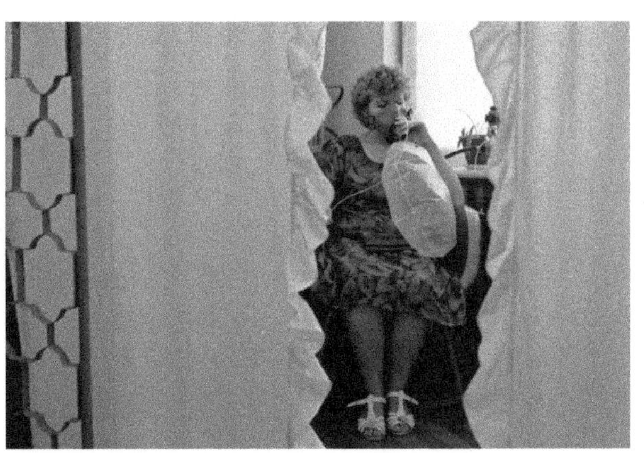
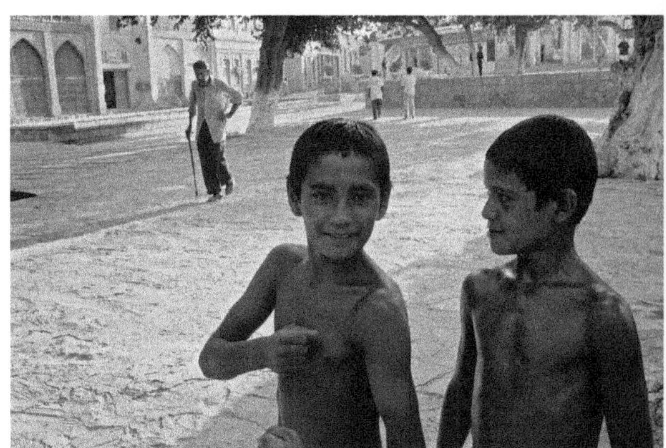
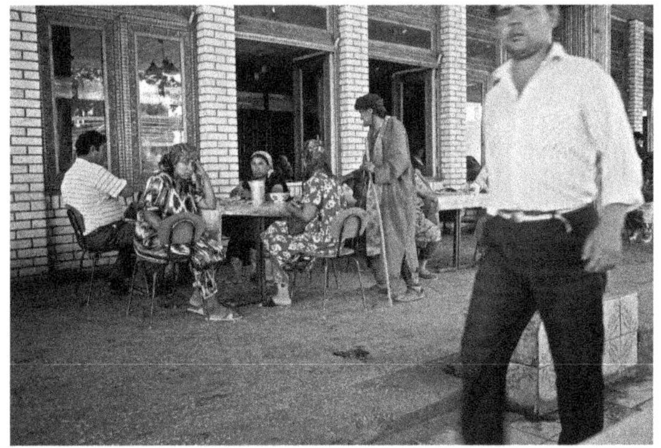
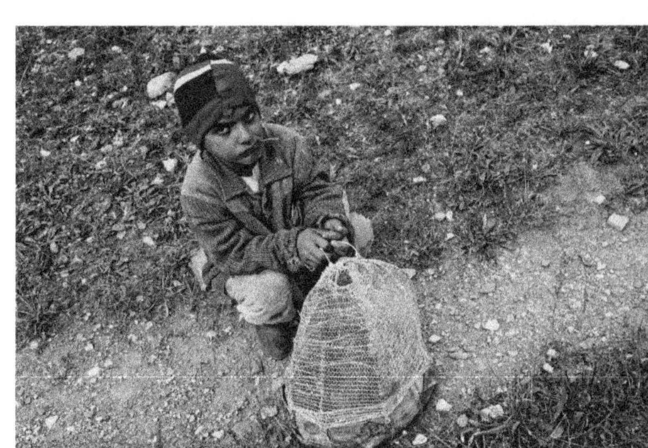
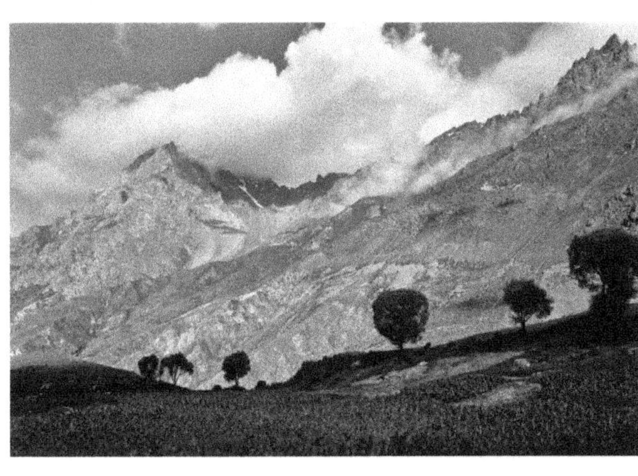
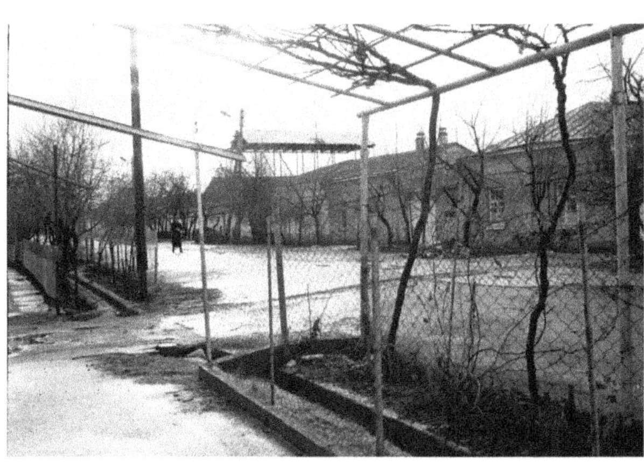

Image manipulation

DISCUSSING WHAT LEVEL OF MANIPULATION is acceptable is usually done with rather broad brushstrokes. For example, debates usually appeal to analogue dark-room techniques to decide what's acceptable or not. Apart from being deplorably imprecise, this analogy limits the scope of the debate to the knowledge base of the participants. But today's photographers have very little to no idea what went on in the wet dark-room. Or judges rely on subjective responses - i.e. what they feel - to decide how much manipulation is too much.

Retouching prints, negatives and even colour transparencies, or multiple printing, masking, re-photography, shadow and highlight recovery, using toners for subtle through to strong split-toning effects are all dark-room techniques. All were able create to substantial changes to image appearance and content, including the addition of completely new picture components. Just because some of this work demanded high-level skills and therefore cost a lot meant it did not happen in the mainstream. But for those with generous advertising budgets it was routine work.

Notwithstanding the effect of a knowledge gap, waving at analogies with film-based photography leads to confusion and error because the vagueness allows different parties to appear to agree when, in detail, they hold positions that are different. Alternatively - and worse - the protagonists appear to occupy opposing positions when, in fact, they agree on the basic notions, but these have been calibrated in different ways.

Perhaps worse still, differences in the assessment of the image may become apparent only when a specific image or narrow range of issues is under the judging microscope. This can lead to embarrassing discoveries about how e.g. competition rules were not sufficiently precise or were open to mis-interpretation.

In this chapter I propose a scoring system based on scales of visible differences. These combine to give a measure for our notions of what is allowable in terms of manipulation.

Importance of a metric

This scheme aims to help locate the important points of difference in judgements of photographs. Applying the measure does still call for subjective assessments. But, by placing assessments such as 'just visible', 'clearly visible' on a perceptual scale, it is easier to arrive at rankings that everyone can agree on. It is generally easier to agree on ranking of individual qualities than assessing several factors at once. This can be achieved relatively easily where the original capture and the submitted image can be examined both at the same time.

For example, in photojournalism tonal changes which normalise a non-normal scene are generally accepted. For example, an early morning scene in low ambient light with soft, diffused lighting will record as low in mid-tone contrast. We generally accept that, for pictorial use, a photographer can boost mid-tone contrast in order to bring out details. The strength or effect of the adjustment can vary from the nearly invisible to the clearly visible.

We can agree that adjustments with a certain effect are acceptable for a given purpose e.g. photojournalism. But can we can go on to state that any greater effects that dramatically increase the effect of chiaroscuro (light and shade) will confer values on the image that belong more to the aesthetics of camera club pictorialism that is right to allow in photojournalism.

For the purpose of evaluating images, competitions or institutions may calibrate their metrics by reference to test images. That would be the next step of development. This scheme is not intended to set any standards beyond dispute, but to provide a much firmer basis for discussion than having various judges arguing in vague abstractions about the differences between 'moderate' and 'strong', 'dark-room' or 'beyond dark-room'.

Note

- **The modifier 'allowable'** means roughly "what is permissible, tolerable, admissible, compliant with certain rules or acceptable" and is relative to a given framework of norms. It does not refer to any legal, cultural, aesthetic measure or artistic value.

- It would be lovely to be able to **aggregate the score** for each image and compare it to the allowable sum. This works well for low sums i.e. those intolerant of any manipulation, but could easily t lead to unwanted results where image use is more tolerant of manipulation as large scores can overpower low scores. But competition administrators can set maximum allowable scores in any category.

So, to what extent should image manipulation be allowed? First, we adopt a scale.

I suggest a 10-point scale of 0 (zero) to 9 (nine) as follows:

0 = no change at all between the captured image and the image under review.

1 = minor global changes reflecting differences, for example, between default conversions using different raw conversion engines.

2 = almost invisible change - needing a grader's or printer's eye - for the purpose of correcting to normal values or machine calibration.

3 = just visible change for the purpose of correcting to normal values.

4 = visible or light change for the purpose of visual enhancement; a minor but useful correction.

5 = clearly visible or moderate change for the purpose of visual improvement just beyond normal values, and without visible artefacts.

6 = clearly visible change to make image more appealing with values beyond normal but not unnatural or hyper-real, with small visible artefacts permissible.

7 = obvious or strong change emphasising a feature or quality for purpose of producing a striking image, with values clearly beyond normal i.e. unnatural , exaggerated or hyper-real.

8 = radical change to exaggerate an effect in a feature or quality, with strong differences from parent image.

9 = very radical, exaggerated change for the purpose of graphic effect resulting in image markedly different from parent image, even unrecognisable.

How this works

Let's take three scenarios or work situations in which the extent or degree of image manipulation makes some difference to whether the image is regarded as acceptable i.e. whether it is fit for a particular purpose. Let's keep it simple by aiming for a straight, binary 'Yes' or 'No' decision.

Forensic, scientific or evidence-based recording

Where integrity of the actual capture is crucial as when gathering forensic scene-of-crime records, or scientific experiments subject to third-party scrutiny, we won't allow any manipulation at all. We cannot accept anything that would disrupt the integrity of the record. This also forbids changes to file name, and any metadata. We want to ensure, as it were, as straight and uninterrupted a causal line between the subject and the image as possible.

So we'd want the image to score zero in all changes. For example, we look at Exposure/Brightness to see if that has been altered. If not at all, that scores zero, and we check the next one. If Exposure/Brightness has not been altered at all, Tone Curve will probably score zero too, as will Highlight/Shadow. But White Balance is independent of these, so could be varied. But we don't allow any changes here either, so this should also score zero. In the case of raw files, the conversion should, of course, be at the settings used at point of capture.

In some circumstances, we may wish to allow a small adjustment in White Balance, in which case, we may stipulate that the score for this parameter is allowed to score 1, or 2.

And so on, through all eleven parameters (see from p.122). You may stipulate, for most strictness, that the total score cannot exceed 1. Or you may relax conditions and allow a total score up to 10 with no category allowed to score more than 1.

Fine art, experimental, graphic design

Let's go to the other end of the scale. We may characterise allowable changes as being those that allow almost the visible severing of the link between the original capture and the manipulated image. In short, just about any alternation or change is allowed. In fact we may not even need to know - or have any interest in - how the final image is created or in how it compares with the original capture or captures. These images may score as much as 99, but in practice can score somewhat less as some parameters are likely to be only lightly adjusted.

The short conclusion is that, thus far, the proposed metric is producing the results we expect and adapts different norms and practices. The tougher test now is to see how it performs in the middle range.

Photojournalism, news reporting

The stress test for any image manipulation scoring is how it deals with photojournalism and news reporting. Here, we are prepared to accept a certain level of global change in tone, exposure, mid-tone contrast, white balance and colour balance, and monochrome conversion which all broadly enhance the visual qualities of the image without a substantial deviation from the scene as originally captured.

This context therefore covers the middle ground in which some manipulation is allowed - usually constrained to those which shelter under the banner of 'dark-room effects' - but no more: and not too much. This begs the question of how much is 'too much'. Any metric should be able to offer a crisp answer. It should be able to unpick the bundle of 'dark-room' effects so that, for instance, we can allow some removal of minor capture defects without stepping onto the slippery slope of allowing cloning within and into the image.

For example, if in photojournalism and news reporting we wish to keep scores in all parameters to around 5, we are broadly allowing corrections to enhance visual impact without shifting, distorting, supplementing or abridging content, then a clearly visible application of dodge and burn would clearly score more than 4 or 5. So the controversial Hansen image of World Press Photo 2016 might have scored 8 or even 9 to reflect the fact that the tone changes on the faces of the anguished men suggested

Image manipulation

auxiliary (but non-existent) light sources or nearby reflecting surfaces. Therefore, if World Press Photo forbids scores greater than 4 - 5, a score of 7 or 8 would then press the red buzzer for rejection.

Still in news and photojournalism, if we look at cumulative scores over the eleven parameters, we could allow an image to score a maximum of, say, 50 so long as no single parameter scores more than, say, 7 or 8. This would describe an image which has received adjustments in exposure, tonality, colour and removal of minor defects, and so forth. But it has not transgressed by making a large change in any feature. For photojournalistic use we might judge this image OK in terms of post-processing.

The metric is cumbersome but that reflects the complexity of the job. Also, details will vary with the user and the context (e.g. whether it's applied to a competition for amateurs, or to a journalism award on the world stage).

This metric does offer the advantage in being able capture some nuances that are often confused. For example, while burn and dodge effects are widely acceptable to some degree, this method helps you define just how much dodge and burn is acceptable. It helps to define the difference between a 'minor' dodge effect (not easily noticed) from a 'major' dodge effect (easily noticed, or one suggesting new light sources or reflective surfaces).

For more details of the scoring see Scoring image manipulation, from p.134.

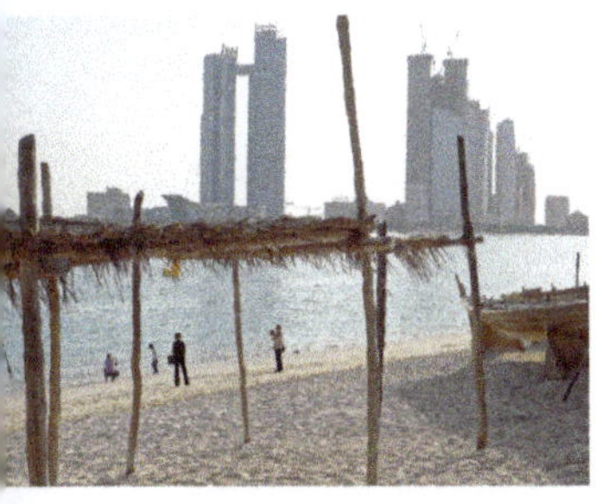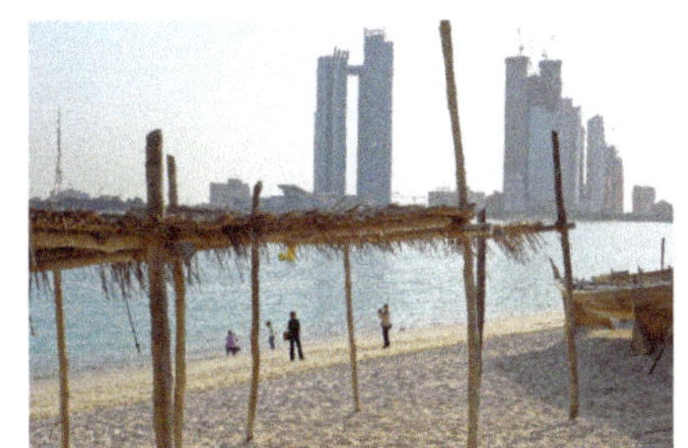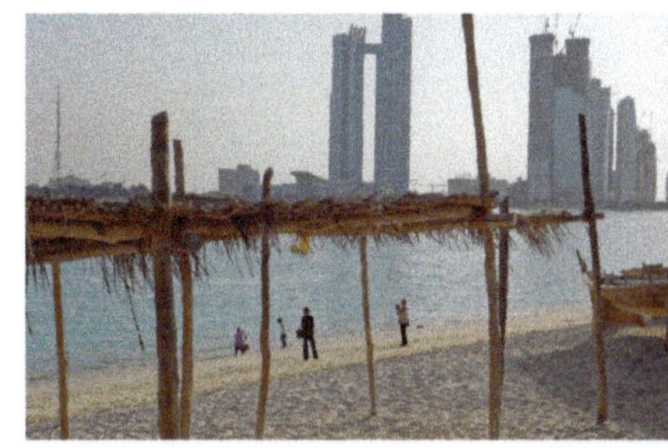
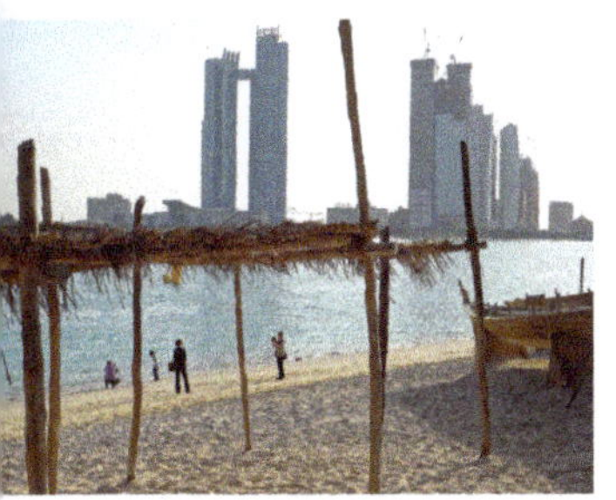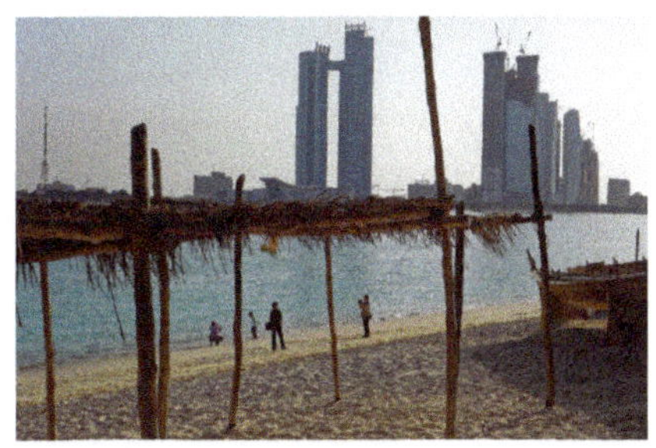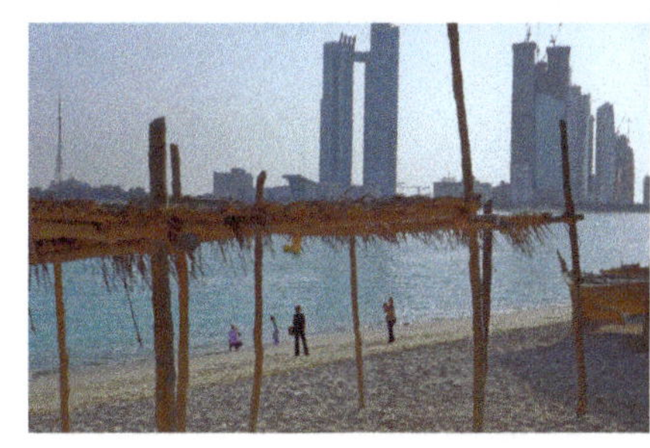
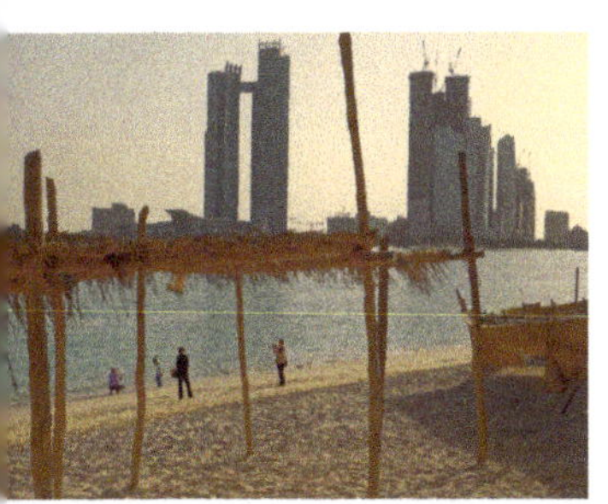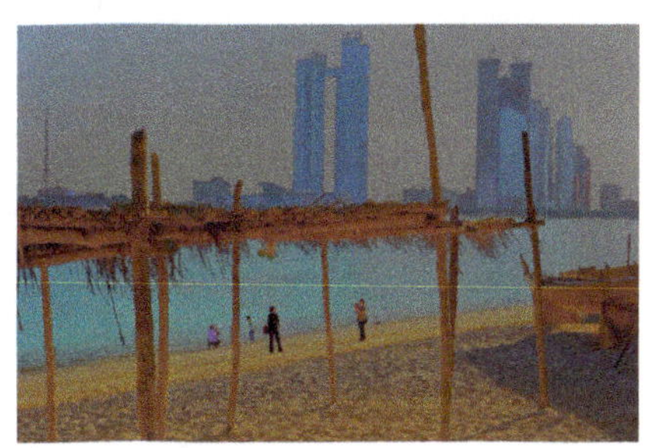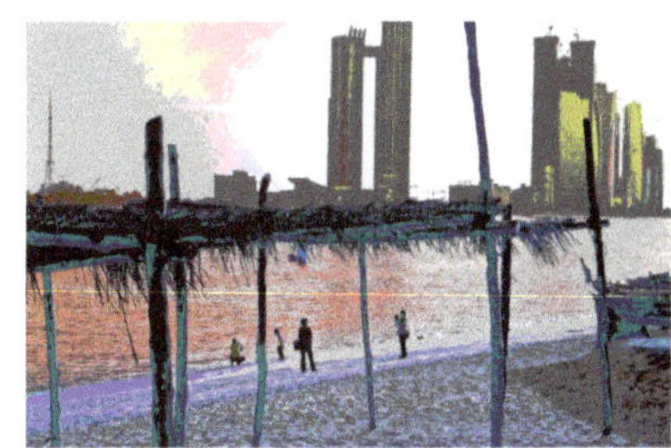

In the sequence of images (*above*) from the original (*top left*) it is easy to see the progressive nature of changes in levels in the upper two rows. In the third row, there is an obvious change in colour balance (*above left*) while there are extreme changes in shadow and highlights (*above middle*) and posterisation (*above right*). If you see any of the first five or six images in isolation, however, it might not be obvious whether had been manipulated out of camera. This is why many competitions ask for the original, out-of-camera, file before awarding a major award.

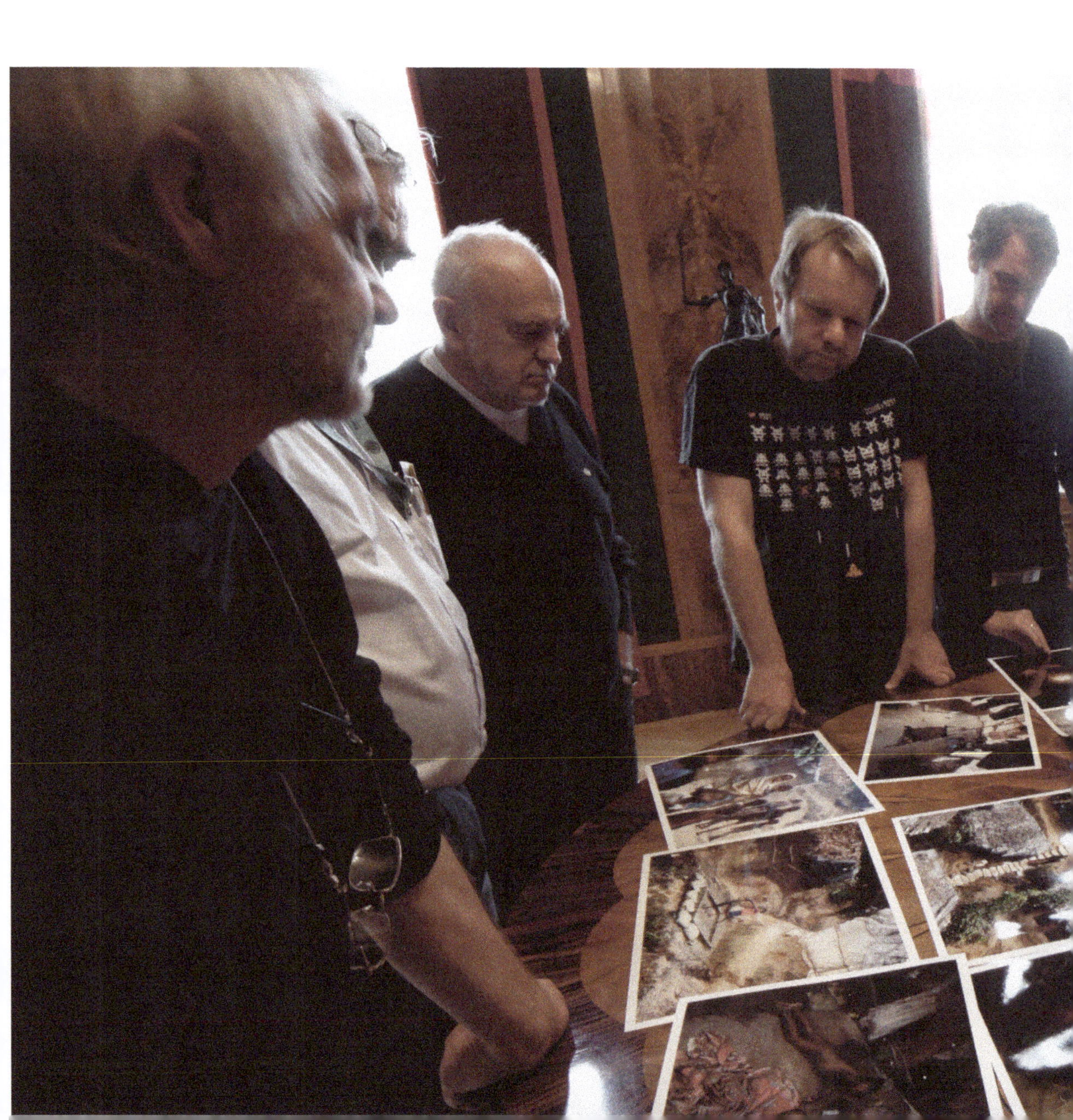

Competition management
Chapter Five

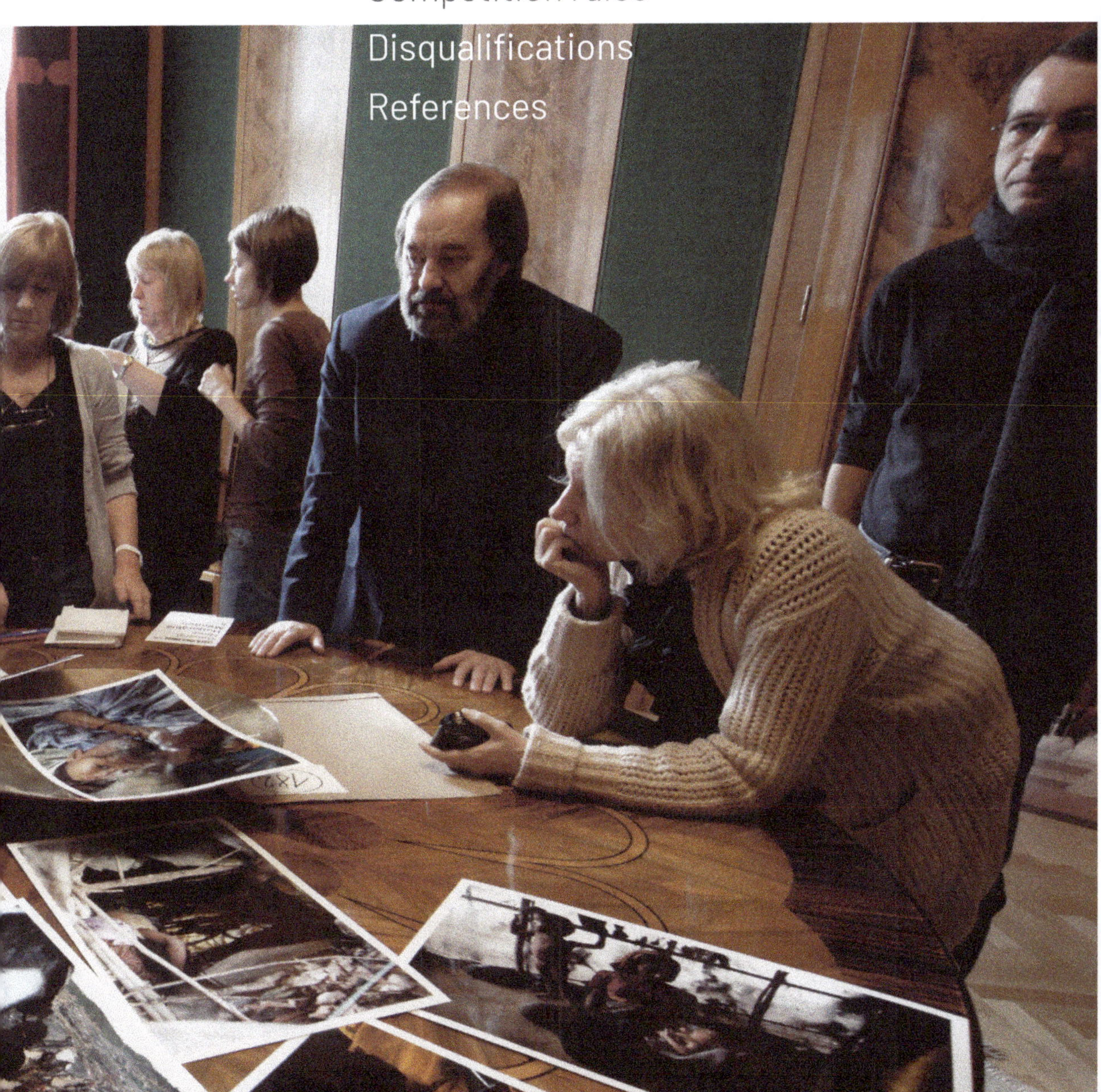

Scoring systems

THERE IS PROBABLY NO UNIVERSAL agreement on any aspect of judging photography apart from this: there no such thing as a perfect system for awarding scores to photographs.

From the simplest 'Yes' or 'No' to the most elaborate scoring system using multiple stages of selection and cross-checks, each has its own advantages and its very own disadvantages. Some systems suit certain types or size of photography competition better than others, while others work best for certain styles of judging or level of judging skill. Some take more time, some need more money and space.

Photography institutions as varied as university-run Masters programmes to local camera clubs to international competitions dealing with over 300,000 entries have all evolved their own systems to meet their needs. Here we look at representative range of systems to help you understand the differences between systems.

The status quo

In the main, when you work as a judge, you will operate in a system that has already been decided and circumscribed for you. If the competition has been running for some years, you can be sure that it has been refined and evolved over the years. Almost certainly not perfect when it was first adopted, it probably isn't perfect even after years of fine-tuning. It is tempting as a newly appointed judge to suggest or insist on changing some details that you find inefficient or unfair. Don't be surprised to be told 'We've tried that before, but ...' followed by some plausible explanation rooted in the competition's or organisation's history. Remember: you're being asked to judge the photographs, not the competition. (By the way, there's a lot to cover, so this is a long chapter. Hang on tight!)

Filtering

Every competition or open-entry event can attract images which are obviously and *prima facie* inappropriate (portraits of family pets for a wildlife photography competition, pornography for a travel photography competition). Or they fail - completely - to comply with the rules or are illegal in some way.

All this even before we look at their merits as photographs. The process of removing, or filtering, these images is more about the management of the competition than actual judging,. Nonetheless, there are areas of overlap that require careful navigation.

A common arrangement is for the competition or award administrators to look at all entries to identify and remove images according to certain criteria. In large competitions, picture editors or assistants may be hired for this initial filter stage.

Criteria for initial filtering or rejection:

- **Images do not comply with technical rules, or are technically illegal** e.g. they are of incorrect size, wrong file format, black-and-white instead of colour. It is essential and straightforward to filter by this criterion. Judges should never have to look at these images at all.

- **Images of inferior technical quality:** badly out-of-focus, badly exposed or with extremely exaggerated colours. Great care is needed here: when there are extremely large numbers of images to review, it is easy to miss an image that appears technically poor but is in fact innovative in its use of the photographic process. Prize-winning images have been chosen from images which looked at first glance to be hopelessly inept and which almost failed to pass this filter. If there's any doubt in the minds of the assessors - often interns or students - it is best to show the images to the expert judges.

Scoring systems

- **Images that are illegal in the country of competition, or in countries where winning images may be shown.** For example, in the majority of countries images depicting nudity of children or minors, or those which incite (or may incite) violence, racial or ethnic hatred are illegal.

  This criterion obviously differs from country to country. And the possibility of the image being shown internationally must now be part of the consideration. This almost always means that the most conservative and careful assessments are needed. All in all, this criterion calls for a lot of care and if there is any doubt, administrators should allow images through for expert assessment by qualified legal counsel and a full discussion between judges should the image reaches final stages of judging.

- **Images that do not comply with basic subject or genre requirements:** for example, they are wrong proportions for a panorama competition; not of buildings for an architecture competition; are formal portraits for spot news. This criterion may call for care: if there is any doubt, administrators should allow images through for expert assessment. For example, what looks like a wild animal acceptable for a wildlife photography competition may in fact be tame or trained but only an expert would know which details to examine or what questions to ask that may reveal the truth.

There are two basic strategies for the first filter:

- **Loose filtering allows all but the most obviously faulty images through:** the technically illegal, those that don't comply with rules in some way, and such like. Obviously, this allows through more images to be assessed by the judges, which increases their work-load and they may complain that they're being asked to examine images which are obviously not going to win. On the other hand, this scheme reduces the load of responsibility borne by relatively untrained assessors, and also reduces the chance of filtering out unusual, or innovative work.

- **Tight filtering aims mainly to reduce the load on the judges.** In some competitions, judges get to review only a proportion - that could be as small as 10% - of the images submitted. This makes for quick and efficient final judging, but of course it relies heavily on the quality of the judgements made by those carrying out the first filtering.

In some competitions, particularly those receiving large numbers of entries, administrators may impose more than one stage of filtering. Past the first filter, judges may decide on which images should go forward to a following round of judging by another set of judges. At this stage, other tests may be applied, such as examining raw files to check authenticity and level of manipulation.

Scoring schemes

We look now at a few scoring schemes and structures for judging that you may encounter, either as a judge or photographer. The general principles that apply here may be extended to the numerous other scoring schemes that are used around the world.

Unanimous vote

The simplest scheme is to choose the top three (or whatever number of prize-winners are needed) from all the entries by unanimous decision. This is easiest if all the images are laid out as prints that can be viewed by everyone all at the same time.
     Selections and rejections are made by public

Scoring systems

discussion, leading to final selections and deciding which is awarded First Prize, which one gets Second Prize, and so on. In this scheme, while first prize requires a unanimous vote, subsequent prizes may be selected by majority vote.

Requirements
- Images need to be output as prints.

- Sufficient space for display of all prints without prejudicing one print over another.

- Judges must be able to communicate comfortably in the same language.

Advantages
- Open, transparent: everyone can see what others are choosing, can listen in to discussions and share opinions.

- Encourages open discussions between judges: helpful for those with different cultural backgrounds.

- It is easy to keep overall view of entries as judges can look back, in their own time, at previously viewed images.

Disadvantages
- Even a relatively small number of entries will require large exhibition or judging space to display all prints adequately.

- Large numbers spread over large spaces are very tiring for judges to review.

- Working in large spaces can fragment judges into small groups or cliques.

- If there are a large number of prizes to award, discussions can become long and protracted.

- Domineering or strong personalities in the judging panel may unduly influence indecisive or diffident personalitiess to follow with group-sanctioned decisions rather than hold to their own, true opinions.

- All judges must be present in the same room for discussions.

In or out

A scheme that is only slightly more elaborate than the unanimous vote is to accept or reject an image. That sounds actually simpler, and in some ways, there can be no simpler. Essentially, it is how photographers select their images for their own use. But the simplicity hides a hive of micro-decisions.

What is important is that in photography competitions, this scheme can be used to judge even very large numbers of images by being applied repeatedly over several successive stages. Essentially, we create a decision cascade.

It works this way: judges view the initial selection, and pass through a proportion of the images. At this first stage, it's usually a relatively large portion of the entries. This portion is then reviewed again, so the accepted images move on to the next stage while the majority of images are left behind, rejected. This will be repeated as many times as needed. A large number of images can be whittled down relatively quickly.

Competition organisers can decide exactly how individual images are accepted in each round of selection. For example, at early stages, if at least one judge wants the image to pass through, then it goes through to the next round. In later rounds, organisers may impose a rule that at least, say, three voices saying 'Yes' are needed for an image to be accepted for the next round. In the final stages, organisers may require that the top prizes are chosen with unanimous voice.

Scoring systems

Requirements

- Careful administration is needed to ensure the correct images that were rejected or accepted transfer to the next stage of judging.

- If large numbers of pictures are involved, judges must have the skill and experience to be able to make decisions very quickly.

- If more than three judges are involved in the judging, they need to be able to see the same image together at the same time: this usually means working in a darkened room with large computer or projection screen.

Advantages

- The workload on the judges is relatively light because the only have to say "yes" or "no". This reduces fatigue and may allow for longer judging sessions.

- Images that make it to the final round will have been seen several times over by each judge.

- In the final rounds, judges may be given the opportunity by competition organisers to argue the case for keeping an image.

Disadvantages

- Images are seen several times over, which increases workload where there are very large numbers of images to judge.

- Competition organisers need to manage the image database very carefully to ensure the correct images are dropped or passed to the next round.

- Less assertive or shyer judges may not fully exercise their right to vote an image into the next round if they feel they are a lone voice against the majority. This tendency can develop within only a short when they find themselves repeatedly the only voice advocating for images that others have rejected. However, the problem of the lone voice losing independence is one that is common to any judging scheme in which judges can monitor each other's voting pattern.

First past the post

This scheme gives the top award to the image that receives the highest marks or most votes. In this scheme, judges award marks or a score to each image that they view. These scores are collected and accumulated - usually electronically from keyboards - from all the judges for each image. At the end of the judging, all the scores for all entries are ranked so that, say, the five images with a highest score are the winners, ranked in order. It's simply In theory, all images can be scored, then all the scores totalled up in one go. The winners are simply those with the highest score. Some subsidiary judging may be needed to separate images which receive identical scores.

In theory, this is a simple scheme to understand and manage, and it appears to be the most democratic. The main problem is that the way judges apply marks or a score can vary widely. This means that judges who award marks in a conservative way - mostly giving mid-range marks and only occasionally giving high marks - will influence the final choice much less than judges who award generously i.e. with high to very high marks for many of the majority of images. This problem may be reduced through the training and careful briefing of judges and the monitoring of marks.

Another issue which requires careful planning is the scale or number of points used to score an image. Essentially, if you use a small scale of say 10 points, it is more likely that some images will accumulate identical scores. But the difference

Scoring systems

between generous and tight markers - those giving either lots of marks or low marks - is reduced. If you use a larger scale of say, 100 points, the likelihood of two images receiving the same marks, especially high marks, is reduced. On the other hand, it is easier and faster to award marks out of 10 than out of 100.

Some judging schemes mark images in successive stages. Images that score enough to get through one stage of judging are then scored again, perhaps by other judges, until the images with the highest marks survive to the final round.

Requirements

- Judges should be carefully briefed on the voting system to reduce errors due to irregular marking. For example, one judge may regard all the images as being very high quality and so award marks of 70 or above. Another judge viewing the same images may have more experience or be more critical, the result of which is that she awards marks from 50 to above. If generous marking is due to less critical judging, then a preponderance of generous markers could easily obscure or overwhelm the more critical judges. This is how the more hackneyed or obvious imagery ascends to the top spot.

- Competition organisers need to create or licence scoring software or a computerised judging system that is suitable for their use.

Advantages

- Images are selected solely on the basis of their accumulated score: this can speed up the final decision process.

- An analysis of the scoring patterns of each judge may be obtained from the data to help with briefing judges, the refinement of the competition rules, or, indeed, assessing the quality of judging.

- If judges are not expected to discuss reasons for their scoring with other judges, this process can take place online through a website. This means, of course, judges do not have to be in the same room at the same time. In fact, judging doesn't have to take place at exactly the same time and judges can work independently, online.

Disadvantages

- The pressure to get through as many images as possible discourages discussion amongst judges. This tends to favour the more obvious images and Is prejudicial against images which are more subtle, enigmatic or innovative.

- Marked differences in the marking habits of the judges may skew or distort the scoring of images: in general, if scores are automatically calculated, without any discussion, then the judges who give very high scores have a proportionally larger influence on the final results than judges who score conservatively.

People's choice

A scoring much favoured by competitions that value interaction with a wider public i.e. not only photographers, is to open up a part of the judging to the public for them to select a 'people's choice' winner, if not the main one. This part of the competition can be very helpful for increasing public engagement. It also serves as an survey-based gauge for the kinds of images most popular with the public.

The operation can be conducted entirely online for the public to view images and choose their favourite image. Routines written into the website can collect all the scores and nominate the winner for administrators to announce.

- **Care needs to be taken in the web site programming to prevent bulk scoring** or the use of software robots ('bots') to boost the scores for a picture. Competition administrators may rely on analysis of scores: unusually high scores may need to be examined for possible vote rigging. However, if users are required to register with robot capture checks, the measures will introduce a barrier to entry that may reduce participation.

- **The images offered for the people's choice may be chosen by the judges** specifically for the purpose or could be a collection of runner-up pictures. Alternatively, peoples' choice images may be offered from the category winners.

- Where an exhibition is held, the people's choice award can be run both online through the competition website and also offered as part of the engagement activities at an exhibition. For example, organisers may provide tablets or computer terminals for direct entry or visitors could be given cards to fill in and submit. This can be a way to increase the email lists as well.

Long or short scales

Fundamental to any system or scheme for judging images - whether it's the individual photographer, or assessments in college, or international photography competitions - is the question of the most appropriate scale with which to work.

As we've seen, it can be as simple as a binary 'in' or 'out', 'yes' or 'no or as elaborate as scoring on a scale of zero to 100. The key question is the extent to which we can accurately measure the quality or worth of an image; it is not as if we can place a ruler against the aesthetic dimension of an image, or weigh a digital file on scales. There are indirect ways to measure the effectiveness of an image for particular purpose but that is not the purpose of the exercise in competitions. Despite the intrinsic failings - seen in colleges all over the world, in judging rooms, at thousands of camera clubs, as well as in individual photographers studios - we are all busily assigning marks or stars or some grading system to our images.

In fact, this is a problem that affects any attempts to measure any psychological or emotional response - whether it's to a stage play, literary essay, musical composition or any other form of art. Debating this issue could take up much of a textbook on social and psychological measures.

But we must pass up that temptation; we highlight just a few key points:

- **The shorter the scale,** the more likely judges will use the whole of it. Obviously a two-point scale i.e. yes/no is always used in whole. But even a five-point scale can't be guaranteed to be used in its entirety, much less a 10-point scale. As for 100-point scales, these are hardly ever known to be used in their entirety i.e. scores ranging 0 to 100.

- **Short scales - five or 10 points -** are often regarded as limiting because the discrimination or resolution at the highest scores is insufficient to distinguish between images which are only marginally different.

- **Longer scales - up to 100 points -** are widely used in competitions and college assessments. However, there is persistent tendency, that is very difficult to overcome, to use only a relatively small portion of the scale. Most markers and judges are reluctant to score anything at below 40 or to score anything at more than 80. It takes exceptionally poor work to score or fail with a mark below 40 or 50, and only very outstanding work will score above 80. In part, this is because the use of longer scales tends to give the impression that the marking being applied is in some sense an absolute measure. We discuss that important notion next.

Relative or absolute scales

There can be confusion as whether a scale measures quality in some absolute sense or is relative to the sample. This issue may account for differences in marking styles. A scale applied to measure a sample tends to use the whole scale: the lowest marks represent the worst of a sample, the top marks apply to the best.

Suppose the sample is from a class of amateur photographers learning camera skills. A top score of 80% points to wonderful work in the sample: it is better than 80% of the work in the group. That is a relative score. An absolute score may be 40%: in a professional context the shot is barely passable.

If a scale is applied in a absolute way, we would expect the majority of images to score around or above the middle. Extremely poor images will have been filtered out or not even entered, and only the most exceptional work will attract the very highest marks. This is similar to Olympic games scoring for floor routines: all the elite gymnasts score only a few percentage points less than perfect.

- **Judges should be clear** on which basis they are applying their scoring. In general, marks are given as if corresponding to some absolute measure.

- **The reluctance to award high marks increases in proportion to the mark.** This may reflect the fact that very few images to deserve the highest marks, but it has been widely observed that judges in general will hold back from using the top of the scale.

- **The longer the scale, the greater the impact of differences** in the scoring habits and practices of different judges. As mentioned above, judges who tend to award very high marks can disproportionately skew or distort a cumulative mark if other judges mark conservatively or take a more critical view of the overall standard of work being judged.

- **The longer the scales used, the harder it is to find rational grounds for unit differences in scoring.** This is because the difference between, say, 79 and 80 is proportionally very small, in fact, it's hardly visible and it's even more difficult to present any kind of argument. But in some schemes, for example, university degrees, a score 69 is a whole graduate class different from a score of 70.

- **Long scales are useful for increasing the chance that images receive unique totals** when different judges' scores are counted up ... in theory. But if judges use only a small portion of the scale, that advantage is proportionally reduced.

Discussions between judges

The extent to which judges can debate views about images, share their opinions, and the importance given to discussions between judges vary widely between different competitions. Some competitions are judged entirely online with no interaction between the judges at all. In fact it has sometimes been difficult to establish the extent to which images have been assessed.

In others, judges are constantly discussing and sharing opinions. And in some competitions, a part of these discussions may take place in public.

All competitions and awards schemes face the problem of how to balance the obvious benefits of discussion against the costs in time and logistics needed. If organisers and chairpersons of juries gave judges as much time as they would like for discussion, some judging processes could drag on for weeks. Furthermore, some competitions are so large - attracting hundreds of thousands of images - it is physically impossible to give every image decision the discussion time they may deserve.

Declaring interest

If a judge is familiar with an image, knows the author or has an association in some way then they should 'declare interest' and recuse (remove) themselves from the scoring. This is easiest where judges are allowed to talk with each other.

This is good practice as it's only human and natural that if you know someone's work you may tend to give a higher score or a little extra preferential treatment than if the work is unknown to you. Conflicts of interest may be rare in international competitions, but it will come up frequently in regional and club competitions. It is vital for the integrity of the competition as a whole and for maintaining the reputation of the judging panel that all conflicts of interest are declared without hesitation or delay.

Recusal of a judge may affect any cumulative scoring system. The organiser needs to make allowance for the loss of a score in such a case. The other judges may choose to allow the conflicted judge to score. In no circumstances should the conflicted judge provide information about the work that would not otherwise be available to the panel.

Scoring differences

Where panels of judges score images together, large differences in score may give rise to the need to discuss the scoring. If, for example, a difference in scores for an image means that some judges place that image in different classes from others, then the chairperson may call for a discussion. If the differences are very large, strong feelings may emerge. These may take some time to resolve.

Where images are scored jointly, judges who feel the overall score does not reflect justly on the image (too high or too low) may have the right to insist on a full debate. If allowed in early stages, considerable time may be taken up. But if left to later stages, any injustices may be left too far behind to undo.

Here are some points to bear in mind when deciding on the balance between judging a lot of pictures as quickly as possible and giving sufficient time for debate to ensure fair judgements are made:

Advantages:

- Discussions between judges, sharing reasons for decisions and opinions, are useful for training newly appointed or inexperienced judges. Open public discussions, similarly, help educate photographers about the judging process.

- Discussions encourage openness, transparency and encourages a level of consistency between the judges through the sharing of ideas, preferences and visual styles. This is very valuable particularly when judges come from different countries or even continents, and differing cultures.

- Sharing reasons and personal views may reveal if any judges are approaching the judging process from a radically different position to the other judges. This may provide useful insights. Competition managers may have to decide whether to do anything about it, if at all.

Disadvantages

- A common language is needed for discussions. Of course, this is not a problem with local or national competitions, but can be serious issue where international awards bring together judges from different countries. The usual practice is to conduct

Scoring systems

discussions in English, which naturally disadvantages speakers for whom English is a second language.

- Strong personalities or those who express themselves vigorously may exert an undue influence on the more diffident, younger or more shy members of the panel. Or if a judge's culture frowns on disagreeing with the opinions of a senior figure. One task of a chairperson is to ensure the quiet voices get to speak up to ensure all obtain a fair hearing.

- Discussions over images can take a great deal of time, even with a relatively small group of judges. It has been known for judging panel to spend more than two hours debating the merits of just two images. Discipline from both the judges and the chair of the judging panel is needed. Equally, it is important to avoid cutting corners in the discussion just to get the issue decided.

- An important point that's is often not fully acknowledged is that images considered late in the day or towards the end of the judging process never receive as much care and attention as images seen soon after the beginning of judging. At that earlier point in the day, judges have settled in, their eyes are not tired, their minds are fresh and lively. But towards the end of judging - several thousands images later - energies are low, eyes tired and minds are well curdled. It is difficult to engage in a fully fair discussion at that point. Competition managers must make allowance for these psychological and physiological realities.

Scoring image manipulation

SCORING IMAGE MANIPULATION by using a scale of visual assessment is a frontier in photojudging. In this chapter we look in detail at how the scales may be constructed and how they may be applied to each image characteristic that matters to us. (For the general discussion about measuring degrees of manipulation, see Image manipulation from p.106.)

The scheme described here will enable competition or award administrators to brief judges clearly, unambiguously, and with precision. The following list and the descriptions form the core of the scheme. But it is open to be redrafted, added to or simplified by the competition or award managers. Information here is easily turned into a spreadsheet that can be adapted to meet the specific needs of a competition.

Metrics

Each of the scales below refers to one characteristic of the image which can be judged on a scale in order to arrive at a score. They work like the scales of possible responses in opinion polls that ask you to score your answer in a range from 'Excellent to Poor' or from 'Strongly agree' to 'Strongly disagree' with ten steps from one end of the scale to the other. It's in the nature of the photographic metrics that some - such as exposure - allow some detail or resolution. Whereas while others - such as defect removal - tend to be more coarse in response.

It would be useful for each competition to create a visual reference for some of the key points in the score. Particular attention should be paid to the point at which a certain image manipulation is regarded as unacceptable within the competition's rules.

1   Exposure/Brightness

Overall lightness plus mid-tone value: At 0 we would not allow corrections even if the parent image is badly exposed, 10 allows for extreme change

- **5**   allows capture errors to be corrected to normalise image i.e. spread Levels histogram to fill the range;

- **6-8** allows increasingly exaggerated effects

- **7-8** for pseudo-high key or pseudo-low key;

- **9**   allows heavy adjustments to, for example, Levels to make extremely dark or very light.

2   Tone curve

Shape and position of Curves and white and black point globally applied, with no localisation or local adaptation:

- **1**   allows default conversion of the raw image;

- **5**   allows a curve to boost mid-tone contrast;

- **6**   allows boost in contrast to enhance contrast compared to original capture;

- **7-8** allows boost in contrast in shadow, mid-tone and highlights to create an obvious, easily visible change from original capture;

- **9**   allows extreme flattening, posterised effects or bi-level curve, even reversal.

3 Highlight and shadow

Adaptive highlight and shadow control or tone-mapping applied over whole image (not burn/dodge or localised tone curve):

- **0** forbids any compensation or recovery even in-camera;

- **1** allows just-visible recovery of highlight and shadow as applied by default raw conversion or low levels of in-camera tone adjustment;

- **3** allows visible recovery but without appearing to alter lighting effect;

- **5** allows visible recovery that maps shadows and bright areas to near mid-tone;

- **6-8** allows strong recovery of shadows and highlights;

- **9** allows exaggerated recovery including edge artefacts and increased saturation.

4 White balance and colour balance

White balance (WB) comprising colour temperature and magenta-green (colour balance) correction:

- **3** allows incorrect WB setting to be corrected in main lighting, even if it distorts another light source;

- **5** allows correction of secondary sources to normal i.e. two or more points of correction;

- **9** allows dramatic change to image WB e.g. to turn daylight balance to tungsten.

5   Colour saturation

Either increase or decrease in saturation in all or specific, limited hue bands.

- **2**   allows slight increase or decrease to render image closer to scene as captured;

- **5**   allows visible increase or decrease to improve photographic effect;

- **6-7** allows obvious increase or decrease for deliberate emphasis or exaggerated effect;

- **9**   allows extreme change - to posterised colours or black-and-white.

6   Noise

Noise reduction applied post-capture to JPEG or TIFF images (some cameras reduce noise as part of raw capture:

- **3**   allows noise reduction just visible at 100%;

- **5**   allows moderate noise reduction visible at 100% with just-visible detail smoothing;

- **6-7** allows strong, easily visible noise reduction or introduction of grain e.g. pseudo-film effect with detail smoothing;

- **9**   allows aggressive noise removal or addition of noise or film-like grain which leads to easily seen smoothing in case of the former, or the easily visible obscuring of detail in case of the latter.

7 Sharpening

Matrix convolutions e.g. USM (unsharp masking) or similar that operate over the entire image:

- **1** allows very light overall, but non-adaptive, sharpening;

- **4** allows sharpening visible only zoomed-in;

- **5** allows just-visible sharpening e.g. for online use;

- **6-7** allows visible, adaptive sharpening with just-visible artefacts;

- **9** allows exaggerated sharpening with easily visible halo artefacts.

8 Local tone

Burn, dodge, local curve and similar localised or brush-limited tonal controls:

- **1-2** allows just-visible changes in tone distribution;

- **5** allows visible changes in tone distribution to enhance the image without suggesting changes in lighting compared to original e.g. enhancing catchlight in eye;

- **6** allows clearly visible effect;

- **7** allows very visible adjustments which also imply or suggest changes in light source or reflecting surfaces e.g. burn in shadows to remove detail;

- **8** allows obvious visible adjustments including easily visible vignetting or reverse vignettes;

- **9** allows extensive tonal changes implying changes in light sources, new light sources or reflecting surfaces or obvious vignette/reverse vignette.

9   Monochrome and toning

Conversion of the red-blue-green capture to black-and-white or monochrome, with or without toning and film-like effects.

- **0** allows conversion to black-and-white by desaturation;

- **1** allows conversion to black-and-white based on the trichromatic response of the human eye;

- **2-4** allow increased emphasis on limited tone bands;

- **5** allows pictorially acceptable results similar to those of black-and-white film photography;

- **6** allows introduction of light toning tints similar to those of light dark-room toning e.g. selenium;

- **7 - 8** allow increasing stronger colours and tonal variation from original e.g. to simulate sulphide, sepia toning;

- **9** allows metal substitution or dye toning (or digital equivalent) e.g. gold, ferricyanide, Colovir resulting in strong colour and tonal changes.

10   Small defects

Clone, rubber stamp or repair effects applied to specific defects such as dust or spots i.e. defects that appear smaller than the majority of objects in the image and that were not part of the original subject:

- **0**   forbids any change, including removal of e.g. dust specks or hair;

- **3**   allows only removal of dust specks;

- **5**   allows removal of just-visible defects e.g. stray hair, but not e.g. freckles or other unwanted element;

- **6-7** allows cosmetic removal e.g. freckles, wrinkles without strongly altering character of face and skin;

- **8**   allows removal of non-essential but distracting element e.g. telephone wires in sky, telegraph pole behind head;

- **9**   allows extensive removal causing an obvious alteration in character of face and skin or unwanted element e.g. figure in background.

11   Cloning

Copying of part of image, whether from the same image or another, to replace parts of the original image:

- **0**   allows no cloning of any kind;

- **1**   allows cloning only to repair or heal minor defects such as spots caused by dust on the sensor;

- **3** allows just-noticeable cloning to incidental or peripheral detail which does not substantially alter content of image e.g. small branch of tree or small cloud near edge of image, tear in background paper;

- **5** allows noticeable cloning to repair error e.g. JPEG or sensor read-out error;

- **6-7** allows substantial change e.g. adjustment of model's pose, tidying up drape of clothes;

- **9** allows any level of cloning from multiple images.

For examples of how these scales might work, see from p.104.

Competition rules

THIS SECTION TAKES APART the bit that everyone has to sign or agree to, but that few ever read with care. This applies equally to photojudges as to photographers.

Many things appear obvious, and often very boring or even pointless. But it is essential reading for everyone involved. If you, as a photographer, fail to notice that you are about to sign away certain picture rights, it may be too late by the time you wake up to your loss. On the other hand, if you, as a judge fail to apply a rule, you could make a decision that is unfair to other contestants who had been following the rule. Or, worse, your decision could lead to controversy that flushes failings into the open, and brings the competition into disrepute.

Explaining rules to judges is an often overlooked part of the briefing for judges. Furthermore, understanding the purpose of different parts of the rules may help you draft your own set of rules.

Preliminaries

Rules usually start with preliminaries or general statements that cover items such as the competition's or organiser's name, who can enter, any fee for entry, deadline and so on. It will also explain the nature and motivation of the competition. If you read nothing else, read this first and primary set of clauses.

'By entering the Competition you hereby accept these Competition Rules and the Terms and Conditions.'

- The bare, simple fact of submitting images and entering may mean you agree to the rules, whether you sign any document or not. Furthermore you agree to every single clause in the Rules, whether you've read them, whether you've understood them or not. If the language of the competition rules is not your first language, it is your responsibility to ensure you fully understand the rules before submitting your pictures.

'The Competition is open to all members of the public.'

- Age, nationality, professional status are not defined for this competition. Note that 'public' may imply that anyone professionally engaged in the competition organisation, promotion or production are not eligible.

'Participants must be individuals aged 18 years and over at the time of their submission.'

- A condition such as this usually implies (if not explicitly stated) the organisers may require proof of age if nominated a winner. This may be a legal requirement e.g. for payment of prize money. Entrants may have to warrant that they fulfil this condition or their image could be disqualified (see also p.158).

'The competition is open only to professional photographers. The photographer's professional status must be established by providing a document of verification.'

- The limitation to professional photographers is self-explanatory here, but there is an implication that the document of verification is one that must be acceptable to the competition organisers, irrespective of what you might consider adequate proof. If it's not clear what is needed, contact the competition administrators.

Competition rules

'Deadline: Entries must be submitted by 12.00pm (UTC) on 1/1/20YZ.'

- It is obvious that all competitions must set a submission deadline or closing date. What may not be obvious is that in these days of online submissions, that deadline can be made absolute. This means it may actually be physically impossible to submit after the deadline e.g. the website turns off the entry portal.

  It also means there are no excuses for being late. Typically, there is a rush to submit entries in the hours or a day or two before the deadline. If numbers are large, the competition's computer server may simply give up and no one can submit anything - even if the deadline has not yet passed. Photographers must ensure they submit images well before the deadline to avoid any of these problems.

'A non-refundable entry fee of US$50.00 is required from each entrant.'

- Some competitions make a one-off charge irrespective of how many images as submitted. Other competitions may charge per image submitted. And yet others may not charge at all. If you are entering a competition, it is your responsibility to ensure that you pay what you are supposed to.

  Some websites ensure that correct payments are made, but others leave it up to you to pay the correct sum. If you don't pay the correct sum, don't be surprised if you are disqualified. Or your image may not even be looked at, but you'd never know. Furthermore, if you break one of the rules and are disqualified, don't expect to have the entry fee refunded to you.

Image requirements

All competitions place some kind of restriction on the images you can submit. Some restrictions may be very specific, others allow a loose and even creative interpretation. Competitions may scatter requirements and restrictions in different parts of the rules. What is covered here are only some examples of the kinds of requirements and restrictions which may be set by a competition. Altogether different kinds of requirements may be set by competitions that give, for example, different grades or distinctions, as entries may need to comply with administrative criteria such as whether you have passed required levels of certification or points.

'Images must be taken in the year 20XZ.'

- Competitions that are run annually may insist that entries are up-to-date by limiting the time period of photography. The rule is simple enough to understand, but if you missed the previous year's competition you may be tempted to enter an image that is out of date. Worse, you may be tempted to change the EXIF data for the image to comply. Do not do this: prize winning images can be checked for tampering using forensic applications. Expect to be disqualified when found out.

'Entered photos must not contain personally identifiable information about you: watermarks, tags, borders, or logos, etc. added by you.'

- The majority of competitions wish to see only the image itself, and no elaboration such as a frame or border. Competitions will also rule out images that carry any identification such as watermarks of the photographer's name. Some competitions welcome

Competition rules

caption information but that should be contained within the image metadata and never visible on the image itself. Some competitions may also forbid having identifiable commercial logos or trademarks in clear sight in the image.

'File size: images must be 2000 pixels long on the long side. Not more than 5MB per work. File format: JPEG/150 dpi recommended. The standard colour space for the judging process is sRGB.'

- Competitions vary considerably in the specifications they set for image submissions. Some demand images sized to the exact pixel dimensions, and specific JPEG compression level, and even the colour space that should be embedded. Others simply set maximum file size. It pays to follow the image specifications to the letter, with precision. Some competition administrators set up a website capable of checking the specifications of each image to ensure compliance. If you find your images will not upload, it is likely that your images do not comply with the specifications. If you're not sure, ask for help.

'Entrants are not permitted to submit images that: (i) feature farm animals, family pets; (ii) portray captive or restrained animals, animal models; (iii) have been captured using live bait.'

- Some clauses in competition rules function to clarify or eliminate ambiguity. For example, a wildlife photography competition may need to explain that family pets and farm animals are not wild animals. In addition, there may be rules which set age restrictions or limits on the amount or percentage of a model's bare skin that can be shown. In addition the above rule also mentions unacceptable techniques for capturing the images.

'Photomicrographs must be taken using a light microscope e.g. compound or stereoscopic microscopes. All techniques of light microscopy are acceptable. Electron microscopy is not acceptable.'

- Depending on the nature of the competition, there may be very specific rules about how the images are obtained. Note that, while there may be some latitude regarding how these rules are interpreted, it is not for the photographer to decide on the nuances of their interpretation. Competition judges, usually experts in the relevant field of photography, have all the authority to it make their own interpretation and are not obliged to enter into any discussions with photographers. There will be separate rules stating that the judges' decision are final and won't be discussed. This means it is best to leave no room for error by not trying to be clever.

No photo which has won any previous award or any other competition and announced before XX Month of WXYZ may be submitted.'

- Many, but not all, competitions will reward only their own unique prizewinners, not those that have already won prizes. While competitions are designed, broadly, to promote photography and photographers, they also have to promote themselves and that is best done with their 'own' winners. Some photographers will have versions of prize-winning images which may not be exactly the same - known as 'sister shots' or 'similars' - and they may be tempted to enter these.

  At international levels, judges can be highly experienced and be familiar with prizewinners from all kinds of competitions. If a similar or sister shot reminds the judge of a prize-winning picture, you can be sure the image will be examined with the certainty it will be disqualified if the same or sister image can be found in another competition.

Competition rules

One consequence is that if you have an image that you feel is truly outstanding, it is prudent to be careful which competitions you first enter. Winning a minor, local award may disqualify you from a major international one.

'Works that are identical or similar to another submitted work (the "identical or similar works") as well as works including identical or similar works submitted as separate works, are ineligible for submission.'

- Some competitions will go to great lengths to define exactly what is meant by 'similar'. Some may not allow you to make even substantial changes to one image and attempt to present it as a different image. For example, turning a colour image into a sepia-toned version with strong changes in tonality may not be enough for it to be considered a new image that you can submit to the same competition into a different category. As with other rules, assume that if there is any doubt, judges will disallow the image.

'Photos that show offensive content e.g. nudity, violence or any content deemed contrary to religious, cultural or public morals or traditions will be disqualified.'

- Some rules may be set in response to legal, cultural or religious restrictions on competition organisers. As a photographer, waste neither your time nor that of the competition by submitting images that may even remotely offend these restrictions. Remember that judges will always interpret rules conservatively with the self-imposed aim of staying well within their legal, moral, or religious limits.

Ethics

In some competitions, ethical issues regarding the importance of truthfulness and not doing harm to a subject will form the foundation for some of the rules. The genres of news, documentary, and photojournalism place a high premium on the truthfulness of the image. In other areas, such as wildlife, nature and landscape photography, competitions expect to see photographers respect the well-being of their subject or sustainability of the photography.

'Entrants must not do anything to injure or distress any animals or destroy their habitat in an attempt to secure an image.'

- It may not be obvious from the image alone that an animal has been distressed or its habitat damaged, but expert judges may harbour their suspicions. As soon as suspicions are aroused, the image faces an uphill battle to be selected as a prizewinner. If, as the photographer, you can provide information that proves that you have not disturbed your subject, it is worth providing that in the caption.

'Entries to the contest must report the world in a way that is both creative and honest. Entries must not deceive the viewer or attempt to disguise or misrepresent reality.'

- As the ethics of photography are hard to express clearly, many rules governing this area are open to relatively wide interpretation. As with other rules, it remains the photographer's responsibility to communicate as clearly and accurately as possible. In documentary and photojournalism, this approach impacts on all stages of the process from the initial photography through post-processing to caption writing. Photographers must expect their images to be interrogated and investigated with the same level of scrutiny they apply to establishing the accuracy of their own reporting.

'Caption information supplied must be complete, true and accurate.'

- In some competitions, the metadata and caption information supplied with the image is important for verification and authentication. Inaccurate or misleading caption information - however outstanding the photography - or worse, metadata altered with a view to deceive may in each instance be sufficient ground to disqualify the image.

  In specialised areas that may have naming conventions, ensure you follow them e.g. in wildlife species names may need to be given following scientific standards, or geological specimens may need to state chemical composition as well as sample source.

Image manipulation

Digital adjustments including tone and contrast, burning, dodging, cropping, sharpening, noise reduction, minor cleaning work, tone mapping (HDR), stitched panoramas, focus stacking and multiple exposure taken at the same location at the same time may be permitted provided that they comply with the Competition's principles of authenticity. At any rate, if there are any restrictions, their aim in general is to prevent deception of the viewer or the misrepresentation of reality.

'While digital adjustments are allowed, adding or removing objects, animals or parts of animals, plants, people etc., are not.'

- Many things can count as manipulation in photography. Entry rules may focus on issues deemed most important by the competition organisers. For some, the staging or re-enactment of events may be regarded as manipulation, even if this is not achieved by post-processing. Manipulation may of course be taken as the addition or removal of content from the image using post-processing and image manipulation tools. The safest course of action is: don't do it. Modern forensic applications can detect even the tiniest cloning, addition of highlight or the erasure of detail in a digital image.

Provision of originals

Apart from the original submission, photographers whose images reach the final stages are often required to submit their raw files or original un-retouched JPEG files. Do not attempt to tamper or alter these files in any way. There are now several forensic applications that can detect any changes - even at pixel level - that, if found, is likely to lead to instant disqualification.

'Participants are required to provide files as recorded by the camera for all images that proceed to the final stages of the contest. Failure to provide these files by the due date will lead to disqualification.'

- Where a competition has rules against manipulation or simply wishes to verify an image, photographers must be ready to supply the original file. If you receive a request, you can be sure your image is in a finals shortlist. Therefore, should you expect to be on assignment or a long trip when you might receive such a request, ensure that someone back at base can send the file to the competition organisers. Few things are more frustrating than to know your image reach the final rounds but because of poor administration on your part you missed the deadline and you lost out.

'Raw files (e.g. CR2, .ARW etc.), or original JPEGs will be required for authentication. DNG is permitted if this is the camera's native format.'

- We are transitioning from a period during which everyone was supposed to work with raw files, to one in which even some news agencies insist on JPEG submissions. Essentially, you must supply a copy of the original file as it was written by the camera to memory card. In practice, this means that your only interaction with the file that you send in for verification takes place only at the Finder or Directory level of the operating system. The file must be represented as not having gone through any image manipulation or format conversion.

'Shortlisted images will be required as 8-bit TIFF Adobe RGB files suitable for printing. Entries not of acceptable quality will be disqualified.'

- All competitions will promote themselves by distributing winning images in one form or another. Those that produce catalogues or exhibitions will ask for high-resolution files that are much larger than those that were sufficient for the competition judging. Some competitions make very large prints - even posters - of prize winning images, so these must be of sufficient size and quality for exhibition prints or they will be eliminated.

Judging

Some competitions will provide a brief description of the organisation of the judging. Strictly speaking, these are not rules in a sense of setting out the terms and conditions of the competition. However, this section is useful for guiding photographers to ensure that images submitted will align well with the competition aims.

An independent panel of experts comprising a chair and judges ('the Jury') will be appointed by the Competition to select and award approximately one hundred entries in total.'

'The judging process for the contest involves five specialised juries and one general jury, and takes two weeks to complete.'

- These statements are about how judging is managed by the competition. Should there be any changes in the organisation of the judging, they would have no impact on either the validity of the competition nor on photographers' participation.

'The judging panel have the right, at its absolute discretion, to turn down or reject any image without any notice or explanation to the Participant.'

- With rare exceptions - where there's an explicit promise to give feedback - competitions will not enter into any kind of correspondence with photographers relating to how or why winners were chosen or not. It is obvious why this is a practical necessity. Competition organisers around the world do recognise that this measure inevitably reduces opportunities for photographers to learn how to improve. But debates on the judging processes are very much to be avoided.

Competition rules

'The criteria for judging entries is a combination of news values, journalistic standards, and the photographer's creativity and visual skills. In the case of stories and long-term projects, the edit of the material submitted is also taken into account. Entries will be judged on: Originality, Informational Content, Technical Proficiency, Visual Impact.'

- Some competitions offer a few brief words about the criteria for judging. These, again, do not operate strictly as rules but are information offered to help photographers select images for the competition. Without more detail, for example, the different weightings given to each criterion, it is not easy for photographers to use the information to help them select images for the competition.

  Criteria for judging may be used by the competition to reduce numbers of entries by suggesting that photographers assess their images on e.g. informational content or originality before they make their entry.

Warranties

This section of the rules is largely concerned with protecting the competition, the organisers, and any institution or company behind it. For the photographer, this is a very important section to read and accept. For example, a photographer may hold the copyright, but there may be limits on what can be done with the image. These limits may be caused by owners of rights to a person, artwork, commercial product or logo, or location featured in the image.

Essentially, if you submit an image to a competition, you need to be confident that you hold every relevant right, even if you don't know what they might all be.

'Each entry must be the original work of the entrant and must not infringe the rights of any other party.'

- While it is obvious that work submitted by an entrant should be his or her own work, it is less obvious that the work should be entirely the original creation of the photographer.

  This means, amongst other things, that major elements in a picture should themselves be the original creation of the photographer. For example, images based on the appropriation or copying of someone else's image would not be admissible (see below). An features such as well-known logos may also be not allowed.

  There is also the issue of third-party preparation of photographer's work. This is where an agent or agency prepares the work with post-processing - sometimes considerable amounts - to the photographer's original file. Photographers may need to declare that they were author of the entire image chain from capture through post-processing to submission.

'You must provide within XY days of any request for: a signed release of each identifiable person appearing in the photo; a license from the copyright owner of any artwork in your photo; a release from the owner of any private property depicted in your photo as relevant.'

- Where a competition is risk averse, or is required by local laws, photographers may have to provide full documentation that they have all the model, artwork, and location releases needed to avoid any kind of legal action. This means that, even if you give your own guarantees and warranties, you may need to provide what lawyers call a 'belt and braces' assurance. Whatever you do, put away firmly any temptation to provide falsified or fraudulent documents. If you can't provide required documents, competition organisers may assess the balance of probabilities and still make the award. Or they may not.

'The entrant must either be the sole owner of the copyright of the entry or have the permission of the copyright owner to submit the entry. A copy of any such written permission must be supplied on request.'

- Some competitions allow agents, gallery owners or curators to submit on the behalf of 'their' photographers. The requirement is necessary: it has been known for a photographer and his agency both to submit the same image to the same competition ... causing confusion all round.

Grant of rights

This section of the rules may be also called 'Copyright 'or 'Intellectual property rights' or 'Licensing'. For the photographer, this is another 'must read' section. You must decide if the rights you give up, or license that you grant are proportionate and fair.

Responsible competitions do not take any exclusive rights to your images. They will ask only licences for the purpose of promoting the competition or organisation. It has been known for a competition to grab your rights simply in your act of entering. Competitions based on submissions through social media and photo sharing sites may also take more rights than you are comfortable with because the terms of use of these sites (which were agreed to perhaps years ago, and forgotten) usually take precedence over competition rules. Re-read these rules carefully and make your own judgement.

'By entering the contest, the entrant grants a non-exclusive, irrevocable licence to reproduce, publish, exhibit and communicate to the public, by any means and in all media throughout the world.'

- With this kind of sweep-it-all-up clause, a competition obtains use of every single image that is submitted. You should look out for other clauses that limit use to promoting the competition, and that set a time limit on the licence.

  Although the competition is asking for a non-exclusive licence - so you can continue to market your image - if there is no time limit, consider what happens when a commercial client asks you for exclusive use of the image. You will lose that sale as, having entered that image, you can no longer guarantee exclusive use, yet you didn't even win a prize in a competition.

'The photographer grants the Competition permission to use prize-winning material in all media, including online, in relation to the contest, the exhibition, the Annual, and all promotional activities for the Competition. This permission is limited to an 18-month period from the announcement of the awards and applies only if the material is selected by the jury.'

- This rule is an excellent example of a competition obtaining only such licences on images that are really needed to promote the competition itself. This demonstrates a respect for photographers and their livelihoods and does not attempt to grab rights while your attention is elsewhere.

'The photographer grants the Competition permission to use all images selected by the jury for its online archive indefinitely and without any remuneration.'

- It makes sense to allow indefinite licence for an image to be use in an online archive, particularly if the archive is not used for commercial purposes, but for research and education. However, the phrase 'without any remuneration' sends out a bright red light.

Liability

In order to provide more protection for the competition, the clauses relating to liabilities are motivated by business insurance requirements. It also arises from the commercial aversion to legal proceedings. Some of these clauses take in a rather wide range of circumstances that you are agreeing to 'hold harmless 'or indemnify.

In practice, it is unlikely that any competition calls you in on these clauses. The best way to ensure this never happens is to play by the rules and provide information that is truthful and accurate beyond any reproach. Be aware that the innocent phrase 'hold harmless 'may be taken by some courts to mean the same as 'indemnify' - which means you promise to pay legal costs in the case of any - yes any - legal action being brought that names you as a party.

'You hereby hold harmless, release, indemnify and discharge the Competition, and its partners, affiliates, subsidiaries, agents from all liability, claims, judgments, damages, actions whatsoever, arising out of the Competition.'

- This kind of clause may take up half a page if a competition's lawyers are allowed to have their way, and list every possible eventuality they can think of. In many competition rules, this clause is so drafted that it would - or should - put off anyone from ever entering the competition, if they take them at all seriously. Note there may some practical measure of protection by isolation, that is, if you do not live in the country of origin of the competition; but that is not something to rely on.

'The Competition cannot accept liability for any loss of or damage to any entry submitted into the Competition howsoever caused or for any consequential loss or damage.'

- In the past, when photographers sent in physical prints and transparencies, such a clause was essential to protect the competition because of items lost in the post or by courier. In these days of digital, online delivery of images, such a clause is seldom necessary. But if a competition accepts any kind of original artwork or print, then such a denial of liability is standard. This clause also protects the competition against the possibility that an entry is inadvertently missed by administrators and not seen by judges.

'The competition, your submission and the rules shall be governed by and construed in accordance with the laws of Aotearoa/New Zealand.'

- Such a clause is normal in business contracts, but not universal for photography competitions. It states the governing or applicable law for interpreting the rules and may be important in guiding the exact interpretation of the clauses or specific legal terms (e.g. 'copyright'). It may also indicate the country in which any legal action will be heard.

Disqualifications

ANY COMPETITION OR SCHEME that offers substantial reward by way of fame, cash, cameras or other material benefit will attract a number of people - usually a very small number - who will do their best to exploit shortcuts to the reward or slip through loopholes in the system. That is why competitions have to set up rules, and once the rules are set up they have to be observed and enforced where necessary.

The question of disqualifying an image, or a photographer is not a pleasant one, nor one that is very edifying. Nonetheless, it is important for competition managers and judges to be familiar with the issues and to have considered them before taking any action to disqualify an image or photographer.

Legal basis

When the photographer agrees to the rules of the competition explicitly with his or her signature or implicitly in the act of submitting to the competition, she or he is essentially entering into an agreement with the competition organisers. If the photographer fails to comply with one of the terms or conditions of the agreement - i.e. breaks a rule - then he or she is in breach of the terms. This means that any sanctions to be taken against the photographer should be within the scope of the competition rules. As we will see, this sets limits on what can be done about serious or serial offenders.

The fact that the relationship between the competition and submitting photographer is defined by the rules means that the rules need to be drawn up with some care. This is discussed in the section on Competition rules (see above, from p.142).

At any rate, before any action is taken against the photographer - publicly or privately -

competition managers are best advised to give the photographer a chance to explain the circumstances which may extenuate or materially affect any decision.

- Competition managers should first to establish whether the breach of rules was deliberate or not. And if not deliberate, whether the mere fact of the breach is sufficient to disqualify the entry.

- Competition managers should to be confident that their rules are reasonable, clear and can be fully understood by a normal, intelligent photographer. If the photographer's first language is not that of the rules, it is entirely the responsibility of photographer to ensure he or she understands them fully.

Sanctions

Depending on what the competition rules say, there are a number of actions or sanctions which may be taken against a photographer who breaks the rules or who is disqualified.
These include:

- If the breach of rules is discovered before any public announcement of the winners, the image may simply be dropped from consideration. Competition managers may decide whether to inform the photographer or not. If the image provides possible evidence of a criminal act e.g. killing of an endangered animal, managers may be required by law to report the matter to authorities.

- If the breach of rules is discovered (and if the photographer's explanation has not been accepted) after a public announcement is made, the photographer may be stripped of the title. This should be communicated both privately to the photographer, and announced publicly, preferably with a full explanation for the decision.

- If a material prize (cash, camera, air ticket) has been awarded, competition organisers may demand the return of the prize. Organisers may have to that accept bank or courier costs cannot be recovered from the photographer.

Limits

Competition managers, or judges should not pass comment or make official or public criticism of the photographer, however much they would like to name and shame the offender in public. In general, any action taken against the photographer should be within the scope of the rules of the competition.
It follows that:

- Comments regarding the lack of honesty, or integrity or other attempts to shame the photographer publicly should be avoided. Critical comments of anyone which are made public are defamatory unless proven otherwise. Derogatory or critical comments about someone therefore run the risk of opening an opportunity for a photographer to take legal action against the competition. If so, the competition organisers will then be forced to defend. That is a development that is well worth avoiding.

- Unless provided for under the rules, competition organisers should be cautious about blacklisting anyone i.e. creating a list of photographers who are banned or automatically excluded - even if they are repeat offenders. At the first filter stage, it is entirely legitimate to remove any entry the competition does not wish to consider.

- Unless provided for under the rules, competition organisers should exercise caution over sharing with other competition organisers the names of photographers who break the rules. If these names are used to operate a blacklisting of photographers, it may be regarded as an unfair prejudice or restriction on freedoms of the photographer. Even worse, such an arrangement may be alleged to be a cartel illegally operated by all the competitions involved. In some legislations, such actions or their effect may be illegal or dubious. At any rate, no competition manager wishes to have to defend the issue in court.

- Unless provided for under the rules that competitors sign up for, competition organisers cannot fine, place sanctions on or seek recompense from photographers who breach the rules, even if the photographer has caused extra costs or harmed the reputation of the competition.

Books

Picture Editing – discover your best images, improve your photography

ISBN 978-0-473-55903-8 Nuku.Press
PDF: https://tomang.com/product/picture-editing/

Want to be sure to find your shot? Be sure to chose your best! Gain vital skills and insights to improve your ability to find your best images. Powerful and unique resource packed with information, practical tips, visual exercises and professional methods.

100% The Book of Judges

Henk van Kooten/Vincent O'Byrne, Graphistudio 2013

Richly illustrated guide to judging for photographers, with emphasis on club, concours and commercial competitions with summaries of some competitions, and scoring schemes.

Picture Editing (2nd edition)

Tom Ang, Focal Press, 2000

College textbook on picture editing covering commissioning and editing processes, moral issues, copyright and law. Designed for photojournalism students.

The Artists' Bill of Rights Principles

The Artists' Bill of Rights is a project of Pro-Imaging.org, a worldwide professional imaging forum. Link for the following text (gratefully acknowledged) that leads to other information, is at http://www.artists-bill-of-rights.org/bill-of-rights/bill-of-rights/bill-of-rights/.

Copyright & Moral Rights

- 1. Entrants will retain copyright and moral rights in their works. Terms and conditions of competitions must not require entrants to assign their copyright to another party, nor must it be a condition of entry that the entrants moral rights be waived.

- 2. Moral rights are to be respected, i.e. the rules should state that works used will always be credited to the entrant, that credit taking the usual form of the copyright notice, e.g. © year name

- 3. If at any stage of a competition an entrant may be asked to sign one or more documents to remain in the contest or to be eligible for a prize, replicas of such documents, or at least full details of the rights they require the entrant to grant, must be displayed on the competition website terms and conditions page.

- 4. Any rights metadata present in works submitted to a contest will not be removed, altered, or added to by the contest organisers or sponsors. It shall not be a requirement of the contest rules that entrants are to remove metadata prior to submitting works to a contest.

Limited Free Usage

- 1. The sponsors/organiser will only acquire limited usage rights for works submitted to a competition. Limited usage rights means they must be non-exclusive, and usage is restricted solely to promoting the specific competition the works were submitted to, or future competitions where that competition is a recurring one, and no other purpose. This is termed "limited free usage".

- 2.   Winning and shortlisted works can be used to promote the competition in perpetuity subject to the conditions set out on the Bill of Rights page dealing with competition winner's archives.

- 3.   Non-winning and non-shortlisted images can be used to promote the competition, and no other purpose, subject to a time limit not exceeding (3) three years following the announcement of the winning entries for the competition the non-winning and non-shortlisted entries were submitted to.

- 4.   Limited Free Usage includes the production of a competition book and calendar for a contest displaying works entered to one specific contest, along with a credit for each work published in the book and calendar, as long as it meets the (3) three year limit for a final production run as stated in item 3 above and as referred to, again, in the competition winner's archives.

- 5.   Limited Free Usage includes the production of competition merchandise, namely posters and cards promoting the competition providing they are fully credited and meet the (3) three year limit for final production run as stated in item 3 above for non-winning works and as referred to in the competition winner's archives for winners.

- 6.   Competition rules which do not state that the works will be used to solely and exclusively promote the competition will be deemed to be using the works for other purposes, and such other purposes will be deemed commercial usage.

- 7.   There must be a clear statement of the manner in which the submitted entries will be used by the organiser and sponsors. Competitions which have no statements about how works will be used, or statements which are unclear about the extent of usage will be deemed to have failed this condition.

- 8.   Entrant's works to be displayed on web sites shall have a longest side not exceeding 1024 pixels.

- 9.   Note that charities and other non-profit organisations can obtain additional rights providing they adopt the donation principle described on the Artists' Bill of Rights page dealing with arrangements for Charities.

Commercial Usage

- 1.   Excepting the above allowable provisions under Free Usage above, any other usages will be deemed to be commercial usage.

- 2.   For the purposes of clarification any usage that is not directly, solely, and exclusively related to promoting the competition will be deemed commercial usage.

- 3.   If it is the intent of the organiser or sponsor that they may approach an entrant with a request for commercial usage of an entrants work the rules should make clear that the entrant will be free to agree or decline terms and that such usage negotiation will be independent of the competition.

Declarations

- 1.   It is recommended that competitions provide brief biographical information about the judges who will judge the contest. Where for the purposes of avoiding any attempt to influence the judges the current years judges will be anonymous, there could be brief details of the judges used in previous contests. Where it is the first year of a contest and thus it is clearly not possible to name last year's judges, it is recommended that a statement saying that details of the judges will be announced when the competition winners are announced.

- 2. Competitions should list all organisations granted usage rights to submitted works directly resulting from each organisation's association with the competition as a supporter, sponsor, partner, etc.

End Date within 16 months of Start

- 1. The competition must have a specified date on which prizes will be awarded, and that date must not be more than 16 months beyond the date upon which the competition details are first made public. This condition is to prevent free usage for submitted works extending over years simply because an end date for the competition has been set more than 16 months into the future.

Major competitions

Visit these sites to learn how it's highly experienced competition managers put competitions together. A range of rules, presentation of competition aims, ethics and how to submit images can be found here.

Fédération International de l'Art Photographique
(The International Federation of Photographic Art)
https://www.fiap.net
- Comprehensive documentation for distinctions, biennials, world cup and other details can be obtained from the 'Documents' section of this large site.

World Press Photo
http://www.worldpressphoto.org
- Best known for its photo contest, but also an important archive and source of training. The contest rules are a model of clarity and good practice.

Sony World Photography Awards
https://www.worldphoto.org
- One of the world's largest and most prestigious awards welcoming a very broad diversity of images.

Hamdan International Photography Award
http://www.hipa.ae
- One of the most prestigious of competitions, dedicated to supporting photographers and nurturing photography.

Wildlife Photographer of the Year
http://www.nhm.ac.uk
- One of the longest-established photo competitions, with rules and procedures of model clarity despite complicated competition structure.

The Paris Photo-Aperture Foundation PhotoBook Awards
http://aperture.org/photobookawards
- Prestigious award for photo-books. The differences from other photography awards are worth noting.

Index

Index

About Tom Ang

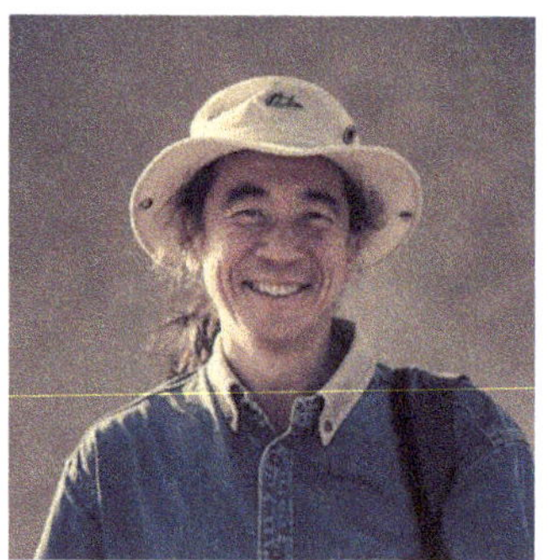

TOM is a leading authority on digital photography, a photographer, author, educator, TV broadcaster, and traveller. He was was awarded the Hamdan International Photography Award for Content Creator in 2019. He won the Thomas Cook award for Best Illustrated Travel Book for his photography of the Marco Polo Expedition which pioneered the modern Silk Road crossing from Europe to China.

He has worked as a magazine editor, picture editor, technical journalist, has exhibited internationally and was a university senior lecturer and course leader in photography for over twelve years during which time he pioneered academic links in the former Soviet Central Asia.

Amongst his 40+ books on photography is the award-winning *Photography - the definitive visual history*, his best-selling *Digital Photographer's Handbook* which has sold over 700,000 copies and translated into twenty languages and the award-winning *Digital Photography Masterclass*. The presenter for two ground-breaking 6-part BBC series on digital photography, he also presented and wrote an award-winning 8-part photography series for Channel News Asia, Singapore.

He has led workshops internationally, including London, Cape Town, Salzburg, Budapest, Dubai, Manila, Singapore and Auckland. He is a founding member of Sony World Photography Award, has been jury member for Czech Press Photo, Wildlife Photographer of the Year and Hamdan International Photography Award.

A Sony Digital Imaging Ambassador for New Zealand and GettyImages contributor, he lives and works in New Zealand.

Feel free to email him, and please do visit his web site for information on other e-books, printed books and lots of pictures.

E-mail: tomangphoto@gmail.com
Web site: www.tomang.com

Acknowledgements

This book has its its origins in a request that Riccardo Busi, President, FIAP, made to me to write a guide for judges. Many thanks are also due to the following for their encouragement and help: Mohammed Al Daou (Hamdan International Photography Award), David Tay (FIAP), Gemma Ward (Wildlife Photographer of the Year), Lloyd Spencer, Manolis Metzakis (FIAP), Jimmy A Domingo, Wendy Gray; Magdalena Herrera, Don Schaefer (Campaign Director, Artists' Bill of Rights).

Notwithstanding the above, any errors are all my own work and entirely my responsibility.

Tom Ang
Auckland
2021